Tales from

BEHIND THE STEEL CURTAIN

Jim Wexell

WWW.SPORTSPUBLISHINGLLC.COM

ISBN: 1-58261-536-5

Publisher: Peter L. Bannon
Senior managing editor: Susan M. Moyer
Acquisitions editor: Mike Pearson
Developmental editor: Dean Miller
Art director: K. Jeffrey Higgerson
Cover/dust jacket design: Joseph Brumleve
Project manager: Kathryn R. Holleman
Imaging: Kerri Baker and Dustin Hubbart
Copy editor: Cynthia McNew
Photo editor: Erin Linden-Levy
Vice president of sales and marketing: Kevin King
Media and promotions managers: Courtney Hainline (regional),
    Randy Fouts (national), Maurey Williamson (print)

Printed in the United States of America

Sports Publishing L.L.C.
804 North Neil Street
Champaign, IL 61820

Phone: 1-877-424-2665
Fax: 217-363-2073
Web site: www.SportsPublishingLLC.com

For my wife, Lydia,
and daughter, Samantha,
whose love and affection
have made the world a better place.

CONTENTS

ACKNOWLEDGMENTS

When you're in the newspapers business—and as a freelancer I must stress the plural—you tend to snicker at these acknowledgment pages. They come off as self-important when really you're just bundling your daily work. All anyone wants to do is read the dang book anyway.

Then you write one of these things, and you realize just how many people have gone out of their way to help. In this case, it was necessary because as an 18-year-old in 1979 I was more interested in my next Legion game or getting to the next kegger down by the Youghiogheny River than I was in this or any football team. So in an attempt to devour the whole of this sub-culture, I needed much help these last three months and there are many to thank.

I first thank a couple of my media brothers. The book would have never begun without Mike Prisuta, and it never would have ended without Ed Bouchette.

I believe Bouchette was sent by divine providence. His most useful of useful tips was convincing me to download to disk half of my work and the remainder of the book's raw data exactly two days before the alarming, yet inevitable, crash of my laptop computer.

Dale Lolley is another media brother who not only helped with tips and phone numbers, but also went above and beyond. He carried the load at our website, SteelCitySports.com, in my absence. I'd also like to thank our boss and one of the great Steelers fans, Joe Schrode, for giving me time off, and another one of my co-workers, Jim Russell, for his helpful research. The biggest thanks, though, at SteelCitySports goes out to the subscribers who patiently waited out Steelers mini-camp last spring without our full coverage.

Vic Ketchman, Bob Labriola, Tunch Ilkin, Joe Starkey, and Mike Fabus also went out of their way to provide information and direction. I'd also like to thank sports editors, Mike Ciarochi, Terry Shields, Alan Robinson and Eric Knopsnyder for giving me enough breathing room to complete this project.

Of course, the greatest source of information was Joe Gordon, the former director of media relations with the Steelers. He's kept up with the former players, coaches, scouts and administrators, and their respect for his name was obvious in the alacrity with which they responded.

Thanks also to the Steelers' current PR department, particularly Ron Wahl for convincing Joe Greene the interview would not be too painful. Your staff is also first rate, Ron. Thanks to Dave Lockett, Vicki Iuni and Brett Martz for their help.

Speaking of help, Ralph McIntyre showed up just in time. So did Doug Hice, Jimmy Caligiuri and Jerry Vernail. Thanks, guys. Tianda Blount, thanks for allowing me to show up.

The encouragement of family and friends was vital. Beyond that, thanks go to my wife, Lydia, for keeping the deck clear. Any writer will tell you how important that is. Dad also came through with an emergency laptop. I can bet with confidence he never expected to see that sentence anywhere. Mom, thanks for knowing how to use it.

Special thanks goes to my sister, Dr. Kris Ruppert, whose medical knowledge helped us through a family crisis during the project.

Members of the Steelers were also helpful, particularly Mark Gorscak, who provided necessary musical and literary tips. He realized the importance of each in this type of project.

Along those lines, thanks belong to artists such as Wayne Dyer, Jimmy McDonough, James Parton, Roy Blount, Neil

Young, Son House, Jackson Browne, Ken Kesey, Hunter Thompson, Plant and Page, and Chuck Prophet for any full or partial lines, or full or partial styles, or full or partially baked ideas I may have flat-out ripped off. I just thought they fit.

INTRODUCTION

J oe Greene just stood at the doorway to the expansive media room at the new Steelers practice facility on the South Side of Pittsburgh, and he watched us work.

Greene had just been hired to work in the team's personnel department after spending 18 years in coaching. He was preparing for the 2004 draft, and his massive frame filled the doorway as he picked up a conversation with a reporter who'd been around during the glory days.

Maybe Greene had time to do that interview I'd requested.

Or, maybe not.

It really won't be painful, Joe.

"Painful for me or painful for you?" Joe said with half a laugh.

He wasn't about to spend his first month back with the team talking about the glory days. In fact, Greene didn't really want to talk about much at all. Another reporter had requested an interview with Greene about Pat Tillman, whom Greene had coached with the Arizona Cardinals.

"After I'm finished with this," Greene told the reporter, who took a seat a few feet away.

"So, how long did you know Pat?" the reporter asked in an attempt to pass time.

Greene, who was signing items for a team charity, turned sharply. "I told you, after I'm finished!"

The reporter apologized and left the room figuring Greene would speak with him later, but he didn't.

"What's done is done," Greene barked after a second formal request had been made.

Still Mean Joe after all these years.

"That'll be a key interview for your book," Vic Ketchman told me. "Joe, Jack Ham and Terry Bradshaw."

Ketchman works for the Jacksonville Jaguars. He was a beat man here during the '70s. Came out of Kent State just ahead of Jack Lambert and covered every one of the Steelers' Super Bowls. He worked for the *Irwin Standard Observer*, the paper for which I had worked as a teen carrier, then a cub reporter and then as Ketchman's replacement as sports editor.

He'd been a big fish in a little pond. The awards announcement sheet from the Pro Football Writers Association of America would look something like this every other year or so:

Vic Ketchman, *Irwin Standard Observer*

Will McDonough, *Boston Globe*

Don Pierson, *Chicago Tribune*

When you research the Steelers' archives, Ketchman's work stands out.

"You want Greene and Ham because the defense was in decline in 1979, and they've admitted as much in the past," Ketchman told me. "You want Bradshaw because of how well he and the offense played that year, but also because he'd hinted at retirement after the Super Bowl.

"That year took a lot out of him. He never had the same fire after that, and he might go into detail."

The 1979 season, of course, was the last championship season of the Steelers dynasty, and it was critical in the sense the Steelers won when they probably shouldn't have, and that it put an everlasting stamp on the dynasty as the greatest of the modern era—as defined by Nielson, of course.

The seventies represented the first era of thorough media coverage and the Steelers dominated. But it was Dallas looking to make amends by the end of the 1979 season. The Cowboys had lost two Super Bowls to the Steelers by a combined eight points and would've certainly been a formidable foe in a third encounter.

Imagine how the course of football history would've changed had the Cowboys and not the Steelers won the 1979 title. The Steelers would've won an outstanding three Super Bowls in five years instead of a mind-boggling four in six. The Steelers, therefore, would not have paraded to Canton nearly as often throughout the next couple of decades. And Steelers fans would miss the whine of Cowboys fans every January after another of their heroes is denied admittance to the Hall of Fame. It's indeed sweet music to the ears of Steelers fans.

No, the 1979 season put an indelible stamp on the Steelers dynasty and its place in history. The Cowboys, of course, were ambushed by the Vince Ferragamo-led Los Angeles Rams in the 1979 NFC divisional playoffs.

The Steelers, who'd been thrashed earlier that season by the San Diego Chargers, 35-7, didn't have to worry about playing the AFC Championship Game in San Diego after the Houston Oilers, without Dan Pastorini and Earl Campbell, upset the Chargers the previous week. The Steelers then beat the Oilers and Rams to claim a title they perhaps—dare I say—did not deserve.

While Bradshaw and company had cranked out the most points in franchise history that year, the defense, the rock of the dynasty, was in steep decline. Ham broke an ankle that eventually ended his career; Greene was a shadow of his former self; the rules changes curttailed the physical style of cornerbacks Mel Blount and Ron Johnson; L.C. Greenwood and Dwight White were past their prime; Mike Wagner was injured and at the end of the line.

Lambert and Donnie Shell were still playing at a high level, but the defense was no longer the Steel Curtain. It was all about offense that year, and the plays made by Bradshaw, Lynn Swann and John Stallworth in Super Bowl XIV hammered the point home.

Even in that Super Bowl, the Steelers were stymied by a Rams coaching staff—sprinkled with former Steelers coaches—who knew the Steelers inside and out. Bradshaw was forced to call the plays at the line of scrimmage, and the game was much closer than anyone had expected.

Did the Steelers win one they shouldn't have? Well, if that's the case, it only made up for the 1976 season. The Steelers believe that to have been their best team, but it was one that didn't end in a championship. You know what they say about the breaks of the game—they even up in the end.

The 1979 Steelers were the last NFL team to win a championship with an entire roster of homegrown talent. With free agency now in the mix, they'll probably be the last. On many levels, there will never be another team like it.

CHAPTER I

BOUNCING OUT OF THE THIRD TITLE:
A BRAZEN CHUCK NOLL RAISES THE BAR

"See everything. Overlook a great deal. Improve a little."

—Pope John XXIII

THE TRUE TOUGH GUY

Jack Lambert once was asked if middle linebackers have to be mean. He shrugged it off as a stereotype and pointed to the guy in front of him.

"Now, Dwight White is pretty mean," Lambert said. "But they don't put that kind of label on a defensive end."

Terry Claus would agree. After the Steelers defeated the Dallas Cowboys, 35-31, to win Super Bowl XIII in January, 1979, Claus went to the hotel near the Miami Airport, where the Steelers were staying, in search of autographs. He was met, according to a letter written to the *Pittsburgh Post-Gazette*, in the hallway by Mike Webster, who offered Claus a beer and introduced him to the players in the room.

"I proceeded to make small talk and ask for a few autographs," Claus wrote. "Then I made the mistake of asking Dwight White. He was furious! He ripped up the paper full of autographs and threw it off the balcony. I remember it falling about 10 stories. I thought he was going to throw me."

It was probably a good thing for Claus that the Steelers had won. Then again, the Steelers had grown accustomed to winning. The guy in charge, though, wasn't about to let them become too accustomed, or worse, comfortable. Chuck Noll was the true tough guy.

The Steelers won their third Super Bowl after a 14-2 regular season in 1978. They lost their two games by a total of 10 points, then outscored two AFC opponents in the playoffs, 77-15, with the defense giving up only one touchdown. But after the win over the Cowboys, Noll told a national TV audience: "I don't think we have peaked yet. I'm looking forward to bigger and better things."

Chuck Noll: The true tough guy of the Pittsburgh Steelers.

THE REACTION?

"We thought we were coming in for practice on Tuesday," said Jack Ham.

Noll wouldn't stand for complacency, particularly in a team that was beginning to age. The Steelers hadn't shown cracks yet, but it was only a matter of time for players such as White, Joe Greene, L.C. Greenwood, Jon Kolb, Sam Davis, Larry Brown, Gerry Mullins, Rocky Bleier, Mel Blount, Mike Wagner and Ham. They would all be at least 30 by the next opening day, with Greene and Greenwood turning 33. So Noll pushed.

"I think every area on our football team has proven itself," he said at the press conference in Miami the day after Super Bowl XIII. "Any help we can get in the draft in the way of competition will serve to spur the veterans we have right now."

And with that, the tone was set for the 1979 season.

BETTER LOOKING EVERY DAY

Terry Bradshaw was 30 and apparently growing younger. In 1978, he completed more passes for more yardage and touchdowns than any other season to that point. He threw for 318 yards and four touchdowns in the Super Bowl, was named the game's MVP and was preparing to play in his first Pro Bowl.

Bradshaw was the best quarterback in the game and proved his cognitive skills in the Super Bowl by not only calling his own plays, as he'd always done, but for his reads of the Dallas secondary. And Bradshaw's best call was the trap by Franco Harris on third and nine that went for a 22-yard touchdown.

"Beautiful," said Joe Greene at the time.

"A great call," said Mike Webster.

The play gave the Steelers a 28-17 lead. Nineteen seconds later, after a fumbled kickoff return, the lead was 35-17. Game over.

"I don't know why Chuck let me call my own plays," Bradshaw wondered recently. But as the host of *Fox NFL Sunday*, Bradshaw doesn't hesitate to criticize modern quarterbacks for their lack of play-calling.

"Please define great for me," Bradshaw said. "How can you say (Joe) Montana's the best ever? He didn't call a play. How can you say Peyton Manning's worth $100 million? He's won one [actually, two] playoff game in five years. And now you're going to ruin your salary cap 'cause he's going to be 20-something percent of the salary cap in Indianapolis. How are they going to block for him? How are they going to keep people together? So I make fun of them, because in real life you make your own choices."

And call your own plays.

"When they back out of the huddle, there's a microphone in his helmet," Bradshaw continued. "It's telling him what to do. All they have to do is call a formation and a snap count, and God, how easy is that? The few times I struggled as a player, I went to Chuck and said, 'Would you call the plays?'

"Now why would I do that? Because it takes all the pressure off me. Somewhere inside, you say to yourself, 'Well, if this game doesn't go the way we want it to go, I didn't call these plays. Chuck did.'"

Would Noll acquiesce?

"He'd call them, and then I had to signal to him that 'OK, I've got it from here.'

"Hey, it's just my way of slapping those guys in the face and letting them know they're not such hot shit. That's the only reason.

"Can I say that? I guess I just did."

Are There Any More Real Cowboys?

NFL Commissioner Pete Rozelle disagreed with official Fred Swearingen's pass interference call on Cowboys cornerback Benny Barnes. Swearingen made the call on a 33-yard Terry Bradshaw pass to Lynn Swan and the penalty gave the Steelers a first down at the Dallas 23. Three plays later, Franco Harris ran 22 yards for a touchdown to put the Steelers ahead, 28-17.

Cowboys fan Winifred Hale had written to Rozelle to protest the call, and Rozelle wrote back. His letter was published in the *Dallas Times Herald*.

"After viewing films of the play, we are of the opinion that there should have been no penalty called on the Swann-Barnes play in the Super Bowl," Rozelle wrote.

The letter surprised Cowboys general manager Tex Schramm but not Coach Tom Landry, who complained about the call at every turn.

After the game, Landry called it "the kiss of death." He ended his postgame press conference by saying, "I'd say it was the ball game for Pittsburgh."

Not that Harris's 22-yard touchdown run on third and nine had much to do with the game. Then there was the fumble on the subsequent kickoff.

"Obviously it was the key play," Landry stressed. "A tight game became lopsided quickly."

The teams played later in the year and Landry wouldn't let it go. In a conference call prior to the October 28 game, Landry said, "We did have the game under control. We felt we were stopping them pretty well and we were moving it better. Then they got the big break with the penalty. They scored, we fumbled, and they scored again, and the game was over."

The complaining wasn't lost on Chuck Noll. A month after Super Bowl XIII, after receiving his ring, he joked about it with Pittsburgh reporters.

"You hear about our new Super Bowl ring?" Noll asked. "It's got a button on the side. You push the button and the top of the ring flips up. Inside there's a tiny tape recorder and you get to hear Tom Landry bitching."

ORIGINAL ZEN MASTER

Phil Jackson received plenty of credit for basically instructing four guys to pass the ball to Michael Jordan. Granted, Jackson dresses smartly and gives a great sideline pose and some pretty zippy postgame quotes, but the father of Zen philosophy, or the art of pro sports maintenance through self-contemplation, is one Charles Henry Noll.

Paul "Bear" Bryant may have turned a generation on to discipline, and Vince Lombardi turned the next wave of coaches into sideline screamers, and Tom Landry added quiet calculation, and Bill Walsh was the genius, but Noll enlightened all of us, as the anti-genius.

"I grew up in a situation where that was taught to me," Noll explained 25 years after the 1979 season. "I'm talking about my high school football, then college football, then the time I spent with Paul Brown and the Browns. All that stuff kind of went through and this is what I learned. I tried to pass it on. And what do they do? They sell what?"

"Whatever they'll buy," said Randy Grossman from a seat nearby.

Noll was dubbed a Renaissance man because he was more than a coach. He was a gourmet cook, wine connoisseur, scuba diver, classical music buff, gardener, pilot. He was so confident, he "bought a plane before he took flying lessons," Rocky Bleier said one time.

Noll played for Brown, who was considered a pioneer in the use of Xs and Os, but abruptly retired as a player at the age of 27.

"I wasn't worth a damn," Noll explained. "I thought I'd gotten all I could out of playing. I thought my life's work was to be entered."

"Life's work" was a term Noll used often throughout his 23-year run as coach of the Steelers. As a player, Noll figured his "life's work" would be in law. He went to law school at night but realized the field wasn't for him.

"Law is built on confrontation," he wrote in *Game Plans For Success*, "while football is built on bringing people together."

Noll also considered a career as an insurance salesman, and felt his training in the field helped him as a coach "because," he wrote, "it taught me how to deal with people. In sales training, we were taught never to take 'no' for an answer. ... Once you heard his objections, you had something to work with. ... You have to be able to sell your program to your team ... and see what can be done to bridge any gaps."

Noll still kids to this day that coaching wasn't his true calling. After four championships, 12 postseason appearances and 209 wins, Noll believes he finally found his life's work.

"Fundraising," he said.

Deep Pep Talks

Chuck Noll didn't worry that his messages might sail over the heads of his players. He aimed high nonetheless. Like his famous pep talk before a road game about the Corinthians sailing to Sparta in the fourth century B.C.

Noll told his players the Corinthians were so committed to victory that when they crossed the sea to Sparta they burned their own ships. The only way they could return home was victorious on Spartan ships.

"That's how committed we have to be," Noll said.

"A lot of times, Chuck was so deep," said offensive lineman Tunch Ilkin. "He would use these stories to make a point. Sometimes guys would be inspired and other times they might miss it."

Sometimes Noll could tell when his message was missing the mark, and he'd change gears.

Early in the 1989 season, after losing to Cleveland 51-0 and to Cincinnati 41-10 in the first two games, Noll wanted to re-set his team's thinking prior to the next week of practice.

"I want you to be very careful about what you hear from the media this week and what you allow through your mind, your computer," Noll started, "because your mind is like a swimming pool."

"Then," said Ilkin, "Chuck started breaking down the chemical composition of what's in pool water, and he was getting pretty technical about it, but he started getting strange looks from some of the guys. He sensed he was losing them."

"In other words," Noll said, his voice rising, "don't let anyone piss in your pool."

"The beauty of Chuck was that every day was a lesson in history, in geography, a vocabulary lesson," said Ilkin. "I remember going straight to my dictionary when I'd get home from practice. Chuck would say things like, 'We have to work on a grass field today in order to prepare for the undulation of the field in Cleveland.' And I'd go home and look up 'undulation.' If you paid attention, you could improve your word power."

Ilkin works in radio and TV in Pittsburgh and is a part of the Steelers' game-day broadcast team.

"Chuck was beautiful, the consummate teacher," Ilkin said. "He is the consummate educator."

IF A MONK FALLS IN THE FOREST ...

Chuck Noll might have been at his best after losses. Rocky Bleier expected a tongue-lashing after a lackluster perform-ance against the Los Angeles Rams in 1978. At the next prac-tice, the players were less than inspired.

"Our heads were really up our butt," said Bleier. "It was one of those practice days where I was expecting a real ass-tearing, where he's going to yell and scream, tell us we're no good and rip us apart. Maybe we needed it and I was looking for it."

Instead, Noll called the team together and told them a story.

"There are two monks. They're on a journey," Noll said. "Sometime on that journey they stopped in a clearing and in the clearing was a stream. On the far side of the stream was a fair maiden who wanted to come across. One monk, without any hesitation, crossed the stream, picked up the fair maiden, put her on his back and set her down. The two monks, in silence, continued on. Sometime further down in their jour-ney they stopped at another clearing. The second monk spun on the first one and said, 'You know it's against the beliefs of our religion to not only come into contact with a person of the opposite sex, but to actually speak to one. You disregarded that fact when you crossed the stream, picked up that fair maiden, put her on your back and set her down.' And the first monk turned to the second monk and said, 'I set her down back there. But you carried her all the way here.'

"All right guys, see you tomorrow at 10 o'clock. Get outta here."

"Honest to God," said Bleier. "The shocked look as I'm looking at the faces of my fellow ballplayers, as they slowly turned and walked back towards the locker room. I could see their heads slightly bent towards the center, in groups of twos and threes and fours, saying to one another, 'What the hell did he just say?' Honest to God."

What did it mean?

The look in Chuck Noll's eyes speaks volumes on the relationship between him and quarterback Terry Bradshaw (12). It was all about winning.

"Well, what he wanted to do was say, 'OK fine, whatever's happened is in the past. Our play is back there. This is a new day.' Well, he couldn't have just said that. That's not Chuck. I relayed my thoughts to him on that many years later and he just got that little, knowing smile on his face and said, 'Got you thinking, didn't I?' And I said, 'Yeah, you did Chuck.'"

THE LEGACY

Tony Dungy joined the Steelers as an undrafted rookie free agent out of Minnesota in 1977 and made the team that year, the first free agent to do so in two years.

Dungy had been the Golden Gophers' four-year starter at quarterback but moved to wide receiver and then safety with the Steelers. He has the unusual distinction of throwing an interception and making an interception in the same game as a rookie before the switch to safety became permanent. Filling in for injured quarterbacks Terry Bradshaw and Mike Kruczek, Dungy completed three of eight passes for 43 yards and the pick against Houston.

Dungy intercepted three passes as a rookie and, as a back-up to Mike Wagner and Donnie Shell, managed to intercept six passes in 1978 to lead the team. Even though he'd started only two games, the total ranked second in the AFC.

But Dungy's ball-hawking skills and voracious study habits did him little good with the Steelers, at least at the time. They traded him later in 1979 to San Francisco for a 10th-round draft pick. He lasted another season in the NFL before beginning a coaching career that, to this point, has spiked in a pair of conference championship games, one with Tampa Bay in 1999 and another with Indianapolis in 2003.

"Basically, everything I do, in terms of coaching and my style and what I want to get done, I borrowed from Coach Noll," said Dungy. "I was there as a player and a coach and that's where I learned about professional football and what it takes to win. His philosophy was you do whatever it takes, you get guys who are willing to do whatever it takes and then you become a fundamentally sound team. You pay attention to details. You don't try to fool people. You don't try to outsmart people. There's a certain way you win in the NFL and that's by execution. So that philosophy I've kept with me ever since then."

Why hasn't Noll turned out more coaches?

"That's kind of amazing to me," Dungy said. "That through all those guys we had there—George Perles, Bud Carson, Woody Widenhofer, Dick Hoak, Tom Moore, just really, really tremendous coaches, Dan Radakovich, that they didn't go on to lead pro teams of their own."

But why haven't more of his players gone on to coach?

"He kind of had a way of making you see football wasn't everything and he encouraged guys to branch out and do other things. Most of the guys had off-season jobs in different fields and he encouraged that, so it was never a situation where you were made to think football was everything, and that if you weren't doing something in football you were nuts. So I'm not surprised at that with the players, but he's had a ton of good coaches.

"I guess because we weren't flashy, just rough and tough and sound, that maybe his coaches didn't get the credit they should have. I never figured that out. Guys from Lombardi's staffs went on to be coaches, and Landry's staffs and later Walsh's staffs. We had unbelievable coaches when I played there and it just didn't seem to come for them. But I certainly would never have been in professional coaching without Coach Noll, and I know I wouldn't have had the success that I've had without getting that background from him because just about everything I do, and the way I do it, has been influenced by Coach Noll."

THE INFLUENCES

Chuck Noll kept a plaque on his desk with a quote from Pope John XXIII: "See everything. Overlook a great deal. Improve a little." It was his approach to coaching.

"Be aware of what is going on around you," Noll wrote in 1995 in *Game Plans For Success*. "Overlook the things that don't matter. Work toward getting better every day. We all could learn from that."

Just as Tony Dungy is quick to credit Noll, Noll is quick to credit his mentors. First on the list is Paul Brown, founder of the Cleveland Browns. Brown drafted Noll out of Dayton in the 20th round in 1953. He played guard and shuttled in plays to Otto Graham for Brown before moving to linebacker.

"From Brown, I learned the value of basics," Noll wrote. "The game really is won by the team that blocks and tackles the best."

Another of his favored Paul Brown quotes: "There is only one way to coast and that's downhill."

Noll's first coaching job was under Sid Gillman, the famed vertical passing guru who once said, "God bless those runners because they get you the first downs, give you ball control and keep your defense off the field. But if you want to ring the cash register, you have to pass."

Noll didn't know it at the time, but Gillman's philosophy would "ring the cash register" in 1979.

"The thing I remember about Gillman was his unquenchable curiosity," Noll wrote. "He was much more the deep thinker. He loved to dissect films of other teams to see what they were doing, to determine if it was a step ahead of what we were doing."

Noll's next stop was the Baltimore Colts, where he coached under Don Shula, his third great influence.

"Shula, like me, played for Paul, so he reflected the same philosophy," Noll wrote. "Don would say, 'We don't want to fool them, we want to beat them.' It was just another way of saying, 'Stick to the basics.'"

It's often said you can't really learn how to win until you understand how to lose. Noll learned that lesson with the Colts. He was part of the staff and team that suffered the greatest upset in Super Bowl history. The Colts were 18-point favorites to beat the New York Jets in Super Bowl III and lost, 16-7.

"The press built us up as one of the great teams of all time," Noll wrote. "All the acclaim may have blinded us a bit. … That game left a lasting impression on me."

The day after the loss, Noll met for two hours with the Steelers, who had just fired Bill Austin. "That was a tough time," Noll said in *The Pittsburgh Steelers: The Official Team History.* "We had just lost the Super Bowl. I wasn't in a great frame of mind. But after meeting with Dan and meeting the family, I knew they wanted to go in the right direction. They were willing to do whatever I wanted. There was no request that was turned down."

"We had some disagreements right off the bat," said then-President Dan Rooney. "That was good, because it showed he would speak up.

"We finally did it right."

IT WAS SIMPLE, REALLY

Chuck Noll has a knack for making it sound easy. He makes you realize that if you keep your feet on the ground and stick to what you know is right, you can accomplish anything.

At the Terry Bradshaw roast to benefit Mel Blount's Youth Home in the spring of 2004, Noll was asked the most basic of questions:

How did you do it?

"There's one very important key—getting good people," he said. "We were fortunate to do that, not only good football players but good people, guys who wanted to succeed and were willing to pay the price to succeed because it's not an easy thing. You take the easy road and goodbye."

Bradshaw agreed, and of course went into greater detail to the amusement of a packed ballroom.

"People have asked us why we were so good," Bradshaw said. "It starts certainly with Chuck Noll, who had the plan, who did it—remember the commercial?—the old-fashioned way. You know, he drafted us.

"He actually looked at tape, got out and looked at the players, talked to them, and made his choice. These were the kind of players he wanted and he drafted us. And then he taught us his philosophy. He had people with character and he had people with heart, not to mention talent.

"We did have a lot of talent. No kidding. Everybody understands that. But all the talent in the world, as we see it structured today in the NFL, doesn't guarantee that a team is going to win the Super Bowl. 'We've got to plug in a player here, a player there.' Well maybe that stuff doesn't work, especially if he's a Deion Sanders. That stuff just doesn't work. So Chuck put it together, and these players stayed together for a long time, and we were good and we got really good.

"When we got ready to play the Oakland Raiders in '74, and Coach Noll had never said this. We'd prepared hard. We'd studied hard. There was no foolishness. Everybody knew their job, their responsibilities. He was a no-nonsense coach. At times he'd kind of cut up and we wouldn't know how to react. Coach Noll, any time he was trying to be funny, we laughed. You were supposed to. And then Joe Greene would say, 'What the hell was he doing?' And I'd always have to keep my finger on Joe because Joe was always the one that wanted to turn on everybody. 'That's our coach and you back off, big guy. I will take you down.'

"But we went out to play the Raiders and Chuck said this: 'We're going to go out there and we're going to beat them.' He had never said that. In five years, he had never said we were ever going to beat anybody. And we were going out to play the Raiders and he said, 'We are going to beat them.' We were an underdog but we went out there and we beat 'em.

"But it started with our coach, with his system and his plan, and he never strayed from it. And we built this atmosphere of winning, of loyalty, of family. I mean, you bring in family and you bring in the common denominator of love. And when you love one another, and you're good, and you're schooled well, and you're taught well, and you have all this self-confidence that he gave us, good things happen. And there, for a long time folks, great things happened."

AND THE BAND PLAYED ON

Tony Dungy's defenses have not only ranked high statistically, they've been studied and imitated. By 2004, seemingly every defensive coordinator in the league had some version of a Cover 2 in his repertoire. Older fans may recognize that defense, that press coverage by the corners backed by an umbrella-like coverage from the linebackers and safeties and nickel back, somewhere from a time gone by.

"I have to laugh when everybody talks about this new Cover 2, the Tampa 2," said Dungy. "Our 1996 defensive playbook was basically a replica of the '76, '77, '78 Steelers playbook. I first saw it in '73. It's certainly nothing new and has stood the test of time pretty well."

A playbook isn't all Dungy has taken from Chuck Noll and passed on for future reference. Dungy also uses the thought processes behind Noll's teaching techniques, if such a thing is possible.

"His whole thing was, 'How do you correct a problem?' You don't just address it," Dungy said. "Everybody pretty much knows what the problem is, and so one of the things he would do, especially with me, as I'd come off the field he wouldn't say, 'Hey, you were wrong. What happened?' It was, 'What did you see? What do you think? You didn't play that particular situation properly. If I can get to your thought process and help you think your way through it, you'll play it right the next time.'

"Sometimes he'd get on guys, but for the most part he was trying to get you to make corrections. That's one thing I always enjoyed about playing for him, and I felt if I ever got into position to coach other guys, I'd want to do the same thing to help them get better.

"How he taught really had an impact on me. That's one of my favorite phrases with players now: What were you thinking? What did you see? What caused you to react that way? As opposed to, hey, you didn't do that right or this properly. Most of the time they know when they made a mistake out there and they're looking for you to help them see why or to help them get it fixed."

Dungy played for Noll for two years and coached under him for eight. He learned what to do as a player and why to do it as a coach.

"He didn't just teach you what your assignment was, he taught you how to win and how to play the game," Dungy said. "I think that's what we all appreciated."

CHAPTER II

THE DRAFT 10 YEARS LATER: FROM "JOE WHO?" TO "GREG WHO?"

"See, Chuck had no discriminations against a down-the-liner, you know a guy who was drafted down the line or a free agent. He didn't discriminate because, listen to this, who was a down-the-liner? Who was an undersized lineman? Chuck Noll."

—Steelers scout Bill Nunn

In Search of ... a Running Back?

With three rings on hand, the Steelers prepared for the 1979 draft off perhaps their greatest full-season performance. While an argument can be made for the injury-plagued 1976 team, the 17-2 Steelers of 1978 actually won the Super Bowl and quite probably were the greatest, and at least the most balanced, Steelers team of all.

They may not have exactly been giddy at the time, but the Steelers could certainly feel comfortable. But there were these nagging numbers: Eleven of the 22 starters would be at least 30 years old by opening day in 1979. Add kickers to the equation, and 12 of 24 starters would be 30 or older.

In September, the oldest units of the team would be the lines. The offensive line had four starters in their 30s: left tackle Jon Kolb would be 32, left guard Sam Davis 35, right guard Gerry Mullins 30 and right tackle Larry Brown 30.

The defensive line had lost Ernie Holmes the previous year. The Steelers traded him to Tampa Bay for 10th- and 11th-round draft choices. Dwight White was 30 and looking to recapture his job from John Banaszak. Joe Greene and L.C. Greenwood were 33.

The Curtain in the Steel Curtain was rusting. In fact, both sides of the line of scrimmage were. Yet, everyone around the Steelers expected them to draft a running back.

"Steelers Eye Running Back as First-Round Draft Pick" went the headline in the *Pittsburgh Post-Gazette* a week before the draft.

Reporter Vito Stellino listed Steve Atkins of Maryland, Willie McClendon of Georgia and Tony Nathan of Alabama as the leading candidates for the Steelers, who would pick 28th, or last, in the first round.

Stellino figured running backs Charles Alexander of LSU, Ottis Anderson of Miami, Florida, Eddie Lee Ivery of Georgia Tech and Theotis Brown of UCLA would all be gone before the Steelers' turn, and he was correct on three counts. Brown was drafted in the second round.

The top columnist in town, the *Post-Gazette*'s Phil Musick, went with the flow. Wrote Musick: "Through the judicious use of hunches, tarot cards, tips, instincts, various crystal balls, loose-lipped scouts, an astrology chart, other writers' hunches, tips taken from the public utterances of coaches and the skill of a palmist from Topeka, I offer to you more discerning followers of the National Football League … a running back who can, in order of importance, block, run, catch. In short, Nathan. If Nathan's gone: UCLA's James Owens.

"What you do here," Musick concluded, "is clip this and have yourself a laugh tomorrow."

Or a quarter-century from then.

Even though both sides of the line were aging, the Steelers sought to draft a replacement for either Rocky Bleier (20) or Franco Harris in the 1979 draft.

GREATEST OF THEM ALL

The Steelers felt they could afford to fish for spare parts in the 1979 draft because the new core of their team had only been in the league five years. In 1974, the Steelers drafted Lynn Swann, Jack Lambert, John Stallworth and Mike Webster. After the draft, they signed free agents Donnie Shell and Randy Grossman.

Arguments have been made for other drafts as the best in NFL history. As a TV analyst during the 2004 draft, Mel Kiper attempted to make a case for the San Francisco 49ers' 1981 draft (Ronnie Lott, Eric Wright, Carlton Williamson, Lynn Thomas). Chicago fans point with pride to the Bears' first-round picks of Dick Butkus and Gale Sayers in 1965.

The Bears picked two Hall of Famers in one round, but the Steelers picked four Hall of Famers with their first five picks in 1974.

As of 2004, no other team has ever selected more than two Hall of Famers in the same draft. In fact, since the draft was instituted in 1936, only nine entire drafts, including the one in 1974, which had five with Dave Casper, have produced more than four Hall of Famers.

"What they did in 1974 was phenomenal," said Steelers director of operations Kevin Colbert. "That class was the best and that was the standard."

Can it be done again?

"To say that can never be equaled I think is selling yourself short," he said. "The problem I see today is there is so much time between the end of the season and the draft and there are so many common workouts now. A lot of times we are at the same workouts. You may have 32 teams represented and you are getting the same information. It comes off too clean in the early rounds."

In other words, a Jack Lambert wouldn't last into the second round today, even though he came from a smaller school such as Kent State.

"Teams actually share workouts," Colbert said. "There are 24 teams that share workout information. We are not one of them. We try to keep as much information to ourselves as possible. With the Internet and all the publicity that this event gets, it's hard to do, but I won't say it's impossible."

CLIP, SAVE, AND LAUGH LATER

Phil Musick probably learned to laugh at himself after the famed 1974 draft. Here's what Musick, the *Post-Gazette* columnist, had to say in the form of analysis after that draft:

"The Steelers seem to have come out of the first five rounds of the draft appreciably strengthened at wide receiver but nowhere else," wrote Musick, who lamented the fact the Steelers didn't draft a tight end, punter or offensive tackle.

"What they did get," he continued," was (Lynn) Swann, who seems to be a sure-pop to help; (Jack) Lambert, who figures to be the No. 5 linebacker if he pans out; and three question marks."

Well, if it's any consolation to one of the finest sportswriters in Pittsburgh over the last half century, those who are paid to analyze talent also missed on Lambert.

"I saw Lambert in an all-star game at Ohio State, at one of the practices," said Steelers scout Bill Nunn. "To be honest, I didn't reject him, but I didn't give him a second-round grade. I thought he was too thin.

Tim Rooney also scouted Lambert for the Steelers. Upon reaching the Kent State campus in 1973, Rooney talked to

Coach Don James, who later coached Washington for 18 years and became the winningest coach in Pac-10 history.

According to the *Post-Gazette*, James told Rooney, "I don't know how I can tell you about this other kid. He's tall and doesn't run fast."

And so Rooney reluctantly went to take a quick look at Lambert.

"I was stunned," Rooney said. "He had those skinny legs, was about 190 pounds, 6-4, and not a super-speed guy. I watched him in practice and I said, 'This kid is growing on me.' I put a real good grade on him. I went out on a limb."

On draft day, the Steelers still hadn't reached a consensus on Lambert. They also liked UCLA linebacker Calvin Peterson. With the clock ticking, Chuck Noll left it up to second-year linebackers coach Woody Widenhofer. He chose Lambert.

THE WRITER WHO SCOUTED A DYNASTY

Long-time Steelers scout Bill Nunn has worn many hats. He's the son of former *Pittsburgh Courier* managing editor William G. Nunn and the father of veteran actor Bill Nunn, who played the part of, among many others, Radio Raheem in Spike Lee's classic film, *Do The Right Thing*.

Nunn also played some football at West Virginia State.

"I was a coward," he said. "I played one year and told the coach, 'You'd better get me off this football field before they kill me and I won't be able to play basketball.'"

Nunn takes great pride in his former basketball teammates, Charlie Cooper and Earl Lloyd. In 1950, they joined Sweetwater Clifton to become the first three African-

Americans in the NBA. Another basketball teammate at West Virginia State was the school's quarterback, Joe Gilliam, Sr.

"Joey was born on West Virginia's campus," Nunn said of the future Steelers quarterback. "So I had a connection there."

It was the first of many to come. But first Nunn turned down an offer to join the Harlem Globetrotters and joined *The Courier*, the famed African-American newspaper, after graduating in 1948.

As sports editor under his father, Nunn covered the African-American colleges and named the Black All-America football team, which held its banquet in Pittsburgh.

In 1967, Dan Rooney convinced Nunn to scout for the Steelers on a part-time basis. In 1970, Chuck Noll convinced Nunn to leave the newspaper field for good after he'd risen to managing editor, and Nunn became a full-time scout for the Steelers. One of his first finds was defensive end L.C. Greenwood (6-6, 215) out of Arkansas AM&N.

"A good, skinny athlete who could run," Nunn said. "He just had athletic ability. And one of the things that helped L.C. for us was (Dan) Radakovich. Had George Perles been the defensive coordinator, L.C. might not have made it here, but we had Radakovich, who understood speed and quickness. So there's different kinds of coaches, too. And Chuck understood that. See, George liked those big, tough, head-buttin' sumbitches who couldn't run, couldn't do shit, right?"

The Steelers took Greenwood in the 10th round of the 1969 draft. The Dallas Cowboys were interested, but the AM&N team doctor told them Greenwood had a bum knee.

"That's why I slipped down the ladder," Greenwood wrote in *The Game of Their Lives*. "I'm sure fate had something to do with my going to Pittsburgh and not Dallas."

Nunn also played key roles in the signing of Donnie Shell and the drafting of Joe Greene, Mel Blount, Dwight White, Ernie Holmes, Frank Lewis, and John Stallworth.

"Very few people talk about Mel," Nunn said. "I thought Mel was a safety, long-legged and all, and Chuck thought he could play corner. We went back and Chuck showed me film and stuff, and Chuck was right, naturally, because Mel's in the Hall of Fame. But I just felt that being as tall as he was he'd have trouble, but the one thing I didn't take into consideration at that time was the bump and run. See, Mel could stymie you at the line of scrimmage."

Nunn's connections with the African-American colleges obviously helped. Then again, those schools were open to any and everyone. But the Steelers—Noll in particular—had an open mind.

"Hey, even with all the draft picks we had, we still had a lot of free agents make it," Nunn said. "See, that's the one thing that Chuck gave to us. See, Chuck had no discriminations against a down-the-liner, you know, a guy who was drafted down the line or a free agent. He didn't discriminate because, listen to this, who was a down-the-liner? Who was an under-sized lineman? Chuck Noll.

"That's sometimes why your better coaches are not stars. They have patience and they can see things, little things that a star can't. It takes a down-the-liner to know the little things, the right steps, the right technique, what you can do to get better. Those are the things Chuck Noll knew. Chuck Noll was a great teacher. And (Bill) Cowher has a lot of that. He was a down-the-liner. He was a special teams player—tough, hard-nosed, aggressive. That's a part of it. Superstars, most of them, don't have the patience.

"Now, I gave you enough. The guy you want to talk to is Art Junior. He was the one who put it together."

*L.C. Greenwood, out of Arkansas AM&N, thought he was going to
be drafted by the Dallas Cowboys.*

ODDS-ON FAVORITES

Art Rooney, Jr., the man behind the 1974 draft board and vice-president in charge of personnel as the 1979 draft approached, was in Las Vegas with his father, Art Rooney, Sr., and Jack Butler, a Pittsburgh man who was the head of the NFL's BLESTO scouting combine. They stopped at the sports book at the Stardust Resort in the spring of 1979 because someone wanted to meet Art Jr.

"He didn't want to meet my dad, he wanted to meet me, and he was a big shot, one of the top oddsmakers in town," said Rooney. "I thought, 'Oh, boy. What's he going to want from me? Inside info? What's this all about?'

"So he came up and told me, 'I've always wanted to meet you. You put together one of the greatest teams in history, and they'll win again next year.' The guy was complimentary and didn't want anything. He just told me the '74 Steeler draft was the best in history and that he thinks we can win it again.

"Now, I saw all the holes we were developing at that point. I saw the age on our lines. Joe and L.C. and Dwight were past their prime. We had some injuries. I really didn't think we'd do it again, but then we did win it. I told my dad after the season, 'Those guys in Vegas are really on the ball.'"

ROCKY'S REPLACEMENT

Steelers halfback Rocky Bleier had a decent 1978 season. He rushed for 633 yards, second in his career to the 1,036 rushing yards he'd piled up in the 14-game 1976 season. But Bleier was entering his 11th season and so the need was perceived.

Everyone in Pittsburgh knew the Steelers were going to draft a halfback.

Yet, while Bleier was a halfback by description, he wasn't the feature back. He was an outstanding complementary player next to fullback Franco Harris, and behind Bleier on the depth chart was Sidney Thornton, a second-round draft pick in 1977.

"Let's say Franco *was* hinting about retiring," said Bleier. "Then maybe you'd say we needed a No. 1 running back. Now, it's a nice compliment for me, but frankly if I were to retire it's not that big of a threat. It wasn't as if I was a 1,000-yard gainer every year."

Bleier was a solid back behind an outstanding line that included four starters aged 30 and older. It was the line that needed the attention, and if not the offensive line, the defensive line.

So why did the Steelers feel the need to draft a running back in 1979?

The question wasn't asked by reporters following the 1979 draft. Word had leaked out the Steelers were looking at running backs and reporters ran with it because: 1.) It was allegedly a deep draft for running backs; 2.) The Steelers didn't hide the fact they were interviewing and giving physicals to running backs; and 3.) A reporter had called a couple of the top linemen expected to be available at the bottom of the first round and neither had been interviewed by or received physicals from the Steelers.

It wasn't popular to second-guess the Steelers at the time, and the reporters had been spoon-fed the information. Since they learned the team was going to choose a running back, they rooted for the running back in order to be right. It became a matter of guessing which one. That's why the only question after the Steelers drafted Greg Hawthorne was: Greg who?

In a takeoff from the famous *Post-Gazette* headline in 1969 that mocked rookie coach Chuck Noll's pick of Joe Greene, the headline above Musick's column on May 4, 1979 read: How, Why the Steelers Chose 'Greg Who?'

Hawthorne had played only three games his senior season at Baylor because of a chipped bone in his hip. While some teams considered Hawthorne a medical reject, the Steelers cleared him at a 100-player exam at Philadelphia's Veterans Stadium. Noll, running backs coach Dick Hoak, director of player personnel Dick Haley and scout Bob Schmitz then flew to Waco, Texas, to test and time Hawthorne. The 6-2, 225-pounder ran a 4.55 40. The Steelers' medical staff examined Hawthorne and trainer Ralph Berlin told the *Pittsburgh Press*, "If he can't play, it won't be because of his hip."

The Steelers felt it was a blessing that Hawthorne had missed his senior season.

"Had he played the whole season, we never would have got him," defensive coordinator Woody Widenhofer said at the time. "The best thing that happened to us was that Greg Hawthorne got hurt."

But then he got hurt again. And again. Hawthorne pulled his hamstring on the first day of training camp. It was the first in a series of injuries that nagged Hawthorne throughout his five seasons with the Steelers. He rushed for 522 yards during those five seasons before going to New England, where he played tight end and wide receiver and caught 34 passes in three seasons. He then played one season in Indianapolis before retiring.

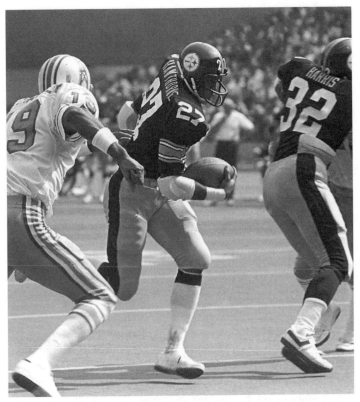

The Steelers' No. 1 pick in the 1979 draft, Greg Hawthorne (27) spent five seasons with the Steelers and rushed for 522 yards.

PASSING ON GREATNESS

The Steelers and 27 other NFL teams passed on future Hall of Fame quarterback Joe Montana—twice. Montana, from nearby Monongahela, Pennsylvania, was drafted in the third round by the San Francisco 49ers and of course led the 49ers to four championships.

"Yeah, we got calls about him," said Art Rooney, Jr. "We got calls from his neighbors, friends, third uncle removed, that kind of stuff. But we had a third-round grade on him, just like the 49ers did and just like probably everyone else did. I'm trying to think why we didn't take him in the third round ..."

The Steelers didn't have a third-round pick. They'd forfeited the pick because of "Shouldergate," a 1978 mini-camp fiasco in which the Steelers had violated NFL rules by wearing shoulder pads and engaging in contact.

"Oh, that's right. Thank God," Rooney said. "I knew there was a reason that didn't turn into a Marino thing for us."

Ah, the "Marino thing." Why did the Steelers pass on Pitt quarterback Dan Marino in the 1983 draft?

"My dad blamed me until his dying day for not drafting Marino," said Rooney. "But it really wasn't my fault."

Here's how Rooney described the Steelers hierarchy of the 1970s: "Noll was the main guy. My dad was the glue. Dan (Rooney) was a phenomenal businessman and great with the league. My thing in personnel was to draft the best available athlete and that fell right in line with what Chuck believed, so we got along great, but he was the main guy."

So it was Noll's call to draft defensive tackle Gabe Rivera instead of Marino?

"Noll loved Marino," Rooney said. "And we had him rated higher than Miami did. And those rumors about Danny? My dad knew every cop in Western Pennsylvania and we really looked into it, but there was nothing serious, nothing like narcotics or anything like that. Dan was just an Oakland kid who got around. He had a great college career, was a little down his senior year, but so was Franco, and we still drafted him.

"We had Bradshaw, of course, and we'd drafted (Mark) Malone in the first round in 1980, but what most people didn't know is that our other back-up, Cliff Stoudt, was the fair-haired boy of the organization. Yeah, Chuck scouted him himself. He had a real good arm, real nice size, could move OK. Still, even with all that, Noll liked Marino so well and so did

I. We really took a long look at him, and in the end it was between him and Rivera and Dave Rimington, a center from Nebraska.

"Well, we crossed Rimington off first because Chuck said he had bad knees and he was right. Then Chuck said, 'This team was built with defense,' you know, with Joe Greene being his first pick and all, and that, 'We can do it again.' So we took Rivera. I said fine, since I wasn't real passionate about drafting Marino.

The Steelers showed little interest in Joe Montana since they already had Terry Bradshaw (12), Mike Kruczek (center) and Cliff Stoudt (left), who was the organization's "fair-haired boy," according to Art Rooney, Jr.

"After the draft, (Don) Shula called Chuck and asked him what he thought about Marino, and Chuck gave him the most positive scouting report he could.

"But my dad never forgave me, and he wouldn't hear anything about Chuck having the last word. I think it might've had to do with Marino getting really friendly with my dad, and besides, how would anyone know the kid we drafted was going to break his back? But even in his last year my dad would see me and he'd say, 'You should've taken Marino!'"

THE REST OF THE STORY

The Steelers might have had the best linebackers in the NFL, and with Dirt Winston and Robin Cole, some quality depth, too. But they felt their linebackers wore down in practice the weeks before playing teams with a 3-4 defense, so in the second round in 1979, the Steelers drafted linebacker Zack Valentine.

They sat out the third round and proved they were serious about upgrading their running game by drafting Russell Davis in the fourth round. He was Michigan's fourth all-time leading rusher at the time, but because he ran the 40 in 4.81 seconds, Davis was considered a long shot.

Or was he?

"You know better than to get me started on 40 times," scout Bill Nunn would say 25 years later. "Randy Grossman couldn't run the 40, but out the cut he was a 4.3. He was quick to separate. That's a part of running, like controlled speed. Franco Harris ran a 4.75 but very seldom got caught from behind. That's competitive speed, so there's different kinds of speed. Then there's some guys, against an Earl Campbell, a lot of guys would out-run him, but they'd take bad angles because they didn't want no part of him. Or Jim Brown, too, right? You'd take the wrong angle and just miss him."

Wide receiver Calvin Sweeney was also drafted in the fourth round. The Steelers might have made their best pick next. In the fifth round they took Dwaine Board, a defensive end out of North Carolina A&T who was nearly as fast as Davis. He was also a three-time member of the Black All-America team, which was selected by Mutual Radio with Nunn out of the newspaper business.

Among the sixth-round picks were cornerback Dwayne Woodruff out of Louisville and place-kicker Matt Bahr out of Penn State. Bahr was drafted to compete against Roy Gerela, who was coming off the worst year of his career. In 1978, Gerela made only 12 of 26 field-goal attempts.

According to Noll, Bahr didn't "have the real strong leg." Noll also said that seventh-round pick Bruce Kimball was drafted to compete with back-up guard Steve Courson, not 35-year-old Sam Davis, who had handled Randy White in the previous Super Bowl.

A couple of tight ends were taken in the late rounds, not only to give Grossman his annual competition, but as insurance for starter Bennie Cunningham, who'd missed 10 games, the playoffs and the Super Bowl the previous season with a knee injury.

CLOSING THE BOOK ON BAD DEALS

The 1979 Pittsburgh Steelers were the last NFL team to win a championship with a roster made up wholly of homegrown talent. With free agency rampant in the modern game, it's safe to say the '79 Steelers will be the last team ever to win an NFL title with all of their own players.

They had some help early in 1979 after closing the book on a couple of awful trades they'd made in 1978.

The Steelers had traded Jim Clack and Ernie Pough to the New York Giants for John Hicks, who, as an offensive lineman at Ohio State, finished second in the 1974 Heisman Trophy balloting. The Steelers were hoping the Giants had mishandled Hicks during his four years in New York, but Hicks never regained his potential and retired in the spring of 1979.

The Steelers made an even worse trade prior to the 1978 season when they traded wide receiver Frank Lewis to the Buffalo Bills for tight end Paul Seymour, who was part of the 1973 "Electric Company" that paved the way for O.J. Simpson's 2,003 yards in a 14-game season. Seymour played five seasons in Buffalo and had missed only one game.

But, while Lewis, a first-round pick in 1971, went on to catch 269 passes in six seasons with the Bills, Seymour flunked his physical during the 1978 preseason and never played a down with the Steelers.

Dan Rooney had hoped the league would step in and force the Bills to give the Steelers a draft pick in 1979 as some form of compensation, but it didn't happen. So the Steelers closed the book on the deal, and on the Bills, that spring.

"I don't think they have clean hands in all of this," Rooney said about the Bills at the time. "I don't think we can believe what they say."

Here's what Seymour told BuffaloBills.com in 2004:

"I was surprised that it was an unconditional trade and that they didn't know I was coming off surgery. In fact, I told them that they were really getting the short end of the trade because I was still recovering. The week before (the trade) I could barely walk, but (the Bills) put me in on a couple of goal-line plays in a game against Detroit and showed the film to Pittsburgh and said that I was OK. Pittsburgh believed it."

Scout Bill Nunn still believes Lewis could've been better than Lynn Swann or John Stallworth, but felt Lewis was too shy in asking Terry Bradshaw for the ball. But on the bright side, the Steelers held on to tight end Randy Grossman, who caught 37 passes in 1978, the most by a Steelers tight end in 12 years.

The trading game, particularly for players, just didn't work for the Steelers. It's little wonder Noll stared down his questioner when asked in the spring of 1979 whether he might trade for players known to be available, such as Terry Metcalf, Jake Scott or Neal Colzie.

"What do you want us to do, go out and get other people's problems?"

SHUFFLING THE COACHING STAFF, FRONT OFFICE

Chuck Noll elevated defensive coordinator George Perles to assistant head coach and moved linebackers and secondary coach Woody Widenhofer to defensive coordinator early in 1979. Also, Dick Walker, who'd been a defensive assistant in 1978, was named the secondary coach.

Perles, 44, became the first assistant head coach in franchise history. His duties were expanded to include offense, special teams and administrative tasks. Bud Carson had preceded Perles as defensive coordinator before leaving, along with Dan Radakovich, after the 1977 season to join another former Steelers assistant, Lionel Taylor, on the Los Angeles Rams coaching staff.

In the front office, director of pro scouting Tim Rooney, who was a cousin of Dan and Art Jr., moved on to Detroit to become the No. 2 man with the Lions behind coach and general manager Monte Clark.

To replace Rooney, the Steelers hired 36-year-old Tom Modrak as a full-time scout. Modrak had graduated from nearby Carrick High School and was a former linebacker at Indiana University of Pennsylvania. He'd been a part-time scout with the Steelers for five years prior to a one-year stint with BLESTO, a scouting combine for several NFL teams.

Fight the Power

Legend has it that Bill Nunn, the Steelers' main link to the African-American colleges in the 1960s and 1970s, was upset with Chuck Noll for passing over quarterback Joe Gilliam through 10 rounds of the 1972 draft.

Not true, according to Nunn. He wasn't mad at Noll. He was mad at the world.

Noll had noticed Nunn sulking in the 11th round of that draft and asked him what was wrong.

"That name up there," Nunn said, pointing to Gilliam's name on the draft board. "That's what's wrong with football."

African-Americans, of course, couldn't play quarterback. At least that was the thinking at the time. But quarterback was just another piece of the evolving puzzle says Nunn, who's watched the times change since covering Jackie Robinson for *The Pittsburgh Courier* in the 1940s.

"There's what I call the match-up game," Nunn said. "It started out with the wide receivers. After awhile you had to get defensive backs because no one could cover the wide receivers. So now you're talking about the match-up game. See what I mean?

"Hey, the last position a black could play was offensive center cause, 'Oh, you had to be smart. You made all the calls.' Now, most of the time the centers were the worst athletes on the team, but you couldn't play offensive line. There were stereotypes, and of course over the years it broke down, but in the beginning ...

"It was like that in all sports. It was in baseball. It was in basketball. The first blacks in the NBA, in 1950, were the guys I played with. And I would've had the first tryout in the NBA, in 1948, with the Knicks, me, right? But I decided to go with the paper because first of all, they didn't want shooters. The first blacks, they wanted them to rebound and give the ball off. That was a part of it. But if you can't relate to Charlie Cooper, it's hard for you to relate to that period of time.

"Just like Jackie Robinson was not the best black baseball player at the time. There were a whole lot better playing at the time. But what Branch Rickey knew was that Jackie had played at UCLA and he felt he could handle the pressure better. It was tough for him to handle the pressure because, see, Jackie Robinson was an evil son of a bitch. He had to bite his tongue.

"The reason we knew all that was you know *The Courier* was in the fight to get Jackie in. See Wendell Smith was hired by Rickey to travel with Jackie. Now you hear all these stories about Sam Lacey, but *The Courier* led that fight.

"A lot of people don't know that either, and one of the reasons for the demise of *The Courier*, other than the fact newspapers in general went down, was we fought causes. And our main thing was we couldn't get advertising—not through the majors because we were fighting them about their hiring policies. Now, we could get the liquor ads and the cigarette ads, but as far the other ads, we fought. Now the reason Johnnie Johnson did it with Ebony was he did not fight causes. He began to get the major advertising. He talked about what's good about America, never what was bad about America."

Unraveling of a Dynasty

As of 2004, Art Rooney, Jr. was still listed as a vice president with the Steelers, but he'd been stripped of his duties as personnel chief after the 1986 season. Drafts such as the 1979 draft helped lead to his brother Dan's decision to fire him.

"You called at the right time," Art Rooney said. "Everybody's been calling lately and going over the '74 draft with me. I've been thinking lately about how it all came apart."

After running a scouting department responsible for the drafting of nine Hall of Famers in five years, Rooney's luck began to run out in 1975.

The Steelers did have a solid draft in 1977, but through 1986 the list of high-round busts became extensive.

"We still had BLESTO and it was still very good," Rooney said. "And we put in a computer system in 1979 that Tom Modrak said was one of the best things we ever did.

"One of the things—now you have to remember, us Rooneys talk in circles and you just have to stay with us for a while and you'll eventually get the story—but one of the things I've been thinking about is that I was always so passionate about the draft, and when I started working with Coach Noll, he said he didn't want arguments, only discussions. But I'll tell you, those discussions got pretty passionate. The stories about our arguments about Franco and those guys, they're all true."

In the 1972 draft, Noll wanted to draft Robert Newhouse in the first round. Rooney talked—argued—him into drafting Franco Harris instead.

"But what happened?" Rooney asked. "Why in the hell didn't we just keep going from there? Sure we began drafting late, but we drafted late in '74, too. I thought I did a pretty good job. Bill Nunn was a very good scout by then. Like I said,

BLESTO was still strong. But we never did draft another Hall of Famer until I was out of there. Why?

"The only thing I've been able to come up with is that after the '74 draft, we didn't have those passionate discussions. They were discussions, but they weren't passionate. Maybe we all thought we were big shots. We still worked as hard as anyone, but the passionate discussions weren't there. We had one with Bradshaw. My dad wanted to trade the pick. He just wanted to do the proper thing, but I was so sold on Bradshaw. But we just had great coaches and great arguments.

"I have gone over it and over it. The set-up we had was still very good, but maybe we all had too much phony respect for each other. Aw, phony's probably too strong of a word, but something was missing. I guess it was those passionate discussions we used to have."

CHAPTER III

SUMMER OF '79:
FIGHTING IN THE STREETS

"Lambert was the embodiment of their image. When he walked into a bar, the whole franchise walked in. And if you took him out, you took out everybody on that team."

—Sportswriter Vic Ketchman

MY DYNASTY'S BETTER THAN YOURS

Chuck Mercein went to Yale, was drafted in the third round in 1965 by the New York Giants, was released in 1967, and was picked up later that season by the Green Bay Packers, who were in the hunt for their fifth NFL championship in seven years and needed a replacement for injured fullback Jim Grabowski.

So Mercein wasn't even a Grabowski, but he did have his 15 minutes of fame. In the Ice Bowl, the game to decide the 1967 NFL championship, Mercein made three key plays during the Packers' final drive over a frozen field, or "jagged concrete" as Mercein called it.

His biggest moment came on Bart Starr's game-winning quarterback sneak. Starr didn't want his teammates tipping off the play to the Dallas Cowboys, so he called a play Mercein was designed to run. Starr instead kept the ball and scored.

The touchdown ended a 68-yard drive that ate up all but a few ticks of the final 4:50 of the game. Of the drive, Mercein would later say: "In the huddle, there was confidence, there was poise, there was a totally professional attitude."

In other words, the exact opposite of what Mercein brought with him to Pittsburgh in 1979. A successful stockbroker on Wall Street at the time, Mercein lost his poise when he ran into Jack Lambert at a bar.

Mercein had lasted another two seasons with the Packers beyond the Ice Bowl, and he'd compiled 105 total rushing yards in three seasons with the team. With those qualifications, he began bragging to Lambert that the Packers dynasty was superior to what the Steelers had accomplished up to that point.

So Lambert whipped his ass.

Or, something like that.

"It is nothing that I'm proud of," Mercein told the *Post-Gazette* a few months later. "It was an immature thing to do. I'm sorry it happened. It was just a silly, boyish thing, one of those 'boys will be boys' things."

So what happened?

"It was nothing," Mercein said. "There was no damage done. Nobody got hurt. It was very forgettable. It was not a memorable conflict at all."

Mercein explained it had begun as a friendly argument that the Packers of the 1960s were better than the Steelers of the 1970s.

Jack Lambert loved to mix it up both on the field and off.

"We were talking football ... there were some comparisons made," Mercein said, leaving the rest up to the imagination.

"I wear my ring with a lot of pride," he said. "I'd hate to dishonor it. I just hope there are no repercussions."

Lambert's reaction?

"Lambert just shrugged," Stellino wrote in the *Post-Gazette*. "It wasn't the first or last brawl for him. But the message was simple. Don't tell Lambert there was ever a better football team than the Steelers of the '70s."

First Anniversary of 'Shouldergate'

A fight between the Steelers and the media broke out in late May of 1979. As in the case of Mercein vs. Lambert, "fight" might be a strong word. In fact, there was probably much rejoicing amongst beat writers when the Steelers closed mini-camp to the media that spring.

The Steelers claimed they did so because the media was "a distraction."

Pittsburgh Press columnist Bob Smizik thought otherwise.

"That's what a spokesman said," Smizik wrote. "But the feeling here is that Noll is doing it strictly for spite."

The Steelers, of course, were still smarting from a 1978 report by the *Press*'s John Clayton that cost the Steelers their third-round pick in 1979.

During the 1978 mini-camp, Clayton, who was not the beat writer from his paper, filled in and was surprised to see the Steelers wearing shoulder pads and engaging in contact. He called the NFL office to inquire about the rules, learned the Steelers had violated them, and reported it.

Clayton was vilified in Pittsburgh, and not only by Steelers fans but by many members of the media. A handful of writers did support Clayton.

"When the story hit the papers," Smizik wrote in 1979, "the town was in an uproar. Not against Noll, who was cheating, but against the poor guy who was merely being a good journalist and doing his job."

To mark the one-year anniversary, Clayton wrote a column about his return to Three Rivers Stadium.

"It was time for the Shouldergate Spy to come in from the cold and return to the scene of the crime," he wrote. Clayton included cutting remarks of a few players, but was surprised by some of the cordial greetings he received at the Allegheny Club, where a luncheon was held.

"I was beginning to feel like Eliot Ness after busting into a speakeasy only to be greeted by 50 smiling faces toasting each other with glasses of milk," Clayton wrote. "I must shoulder the blame for the pads controversy. It was news, which is my job. My job is not to destroy. My job is to report."

Twenty-five years after the fact, long-time assistant coach Dick Hoak explained why Chuck Noll had the Steelers don pads in the first place.

"Chuck said it was because he didn't want anybody to get injured," Hoak told the *Post-Gazette*. "Well, the first day we take them off, we have a receiver dive for a ball and separate a shoulder. That was the whole reason for it; it wasn't because you could get any more done. The reason we put them on was so they didn't injure themselves. We didn't get anything more done with pads on than we do now."

Bradshaw So Lonesome He Could Cry

He was named Super Bowl MVP and called the best quarterback in the game by his coach, but the off season went downhill fast for Terry Bradshaw.

In his hometown of Shreveport, Louisiana, Bradshaw was booed lustily–presumably by the still-hurting Dallas Cowboys fans—while appearing during a benefit country music concert with Larry Gatlin.

Bradshaw was booed after he walked on stage during a Gatlin performance to sing "Your Cheatin' Heart." He was also booed several times during the song despite pleas against it.

"I was shocked," Bradshaw told *The Shreveport Journal.* "I was stunned. I was hurt. I absolutely couldn't believe it. I realize this is a Dallas Cowboys town, but gosh, it's only football."

Gatlin was reportedly furious and told the audience he'd never return.

The incident didn't deter Gatlin from writing a song for Bradshaw, which Bradshaw recorded later that year in Nashville.

A month later, Bradshaw underwent surgery on his right wrist and elbow for the removal of bone chips. He returned to Shreveport after the operation and was slapped on the elbow by an autograph-seeker and an incision was opened. He developed a high fever and that night was rushed to the hospital, where he spent four days for treatment of a staph infection.

On the bright side, Bradshaw's endorsements picked up, as did his speaking engagements. The husband of professional figure skater Jo Jo Starbuck also received an honorary Doctor of Laws degree from Alderson-Broaddus College in West Virginia. A reporter reminded Bradshaw about Thomas Henderson's suggestion at the previous Super Bowl that

Bradshaw couldn't spell cat if he'd been spotted the first two letters.

"Now he'll want to see my thesis," Bradshaw said.

ROOKIE TURNS HEADS AT MINI-CAMP

It didn't take long for the Steelers to identify Dwaine Board, their fifth-round pick from North Carolina A&T, as one of the plums of their draft class.

A 240-pound defensive end, Board drew comparisons to L.C. Greenwood from assistant head coach George Perles, who actually liked Board's intelligence more than his speed, and Board showed plenty of the latter at mini-camp.

The problem for Board, however, was the Steelers were hoping to keep one more linebacker instead of an extra defensive lineman. If all seven veterans—Greenwood, Joe Greene, Steve Furness, John Banaszak, Dwight White, Gary Dunn and Tom Beasley—remained healthy through training camp, Board would be the odd man out on a team looking to make history as opposed to finding starters for the future.

Perles and scout Bill Nunn made glowing public recommendations about Board after the late-May mini-camp. Coach Chuck Noll was less than enthusiastic.

"We've seen him left weights and do stretching exercises," Noll said. "If that's what it takes to make it in the NFL, then he can make it."

PUMPING IRON, SWEATING STEEL

During the season they lifted weights in the boiler room at Three Rivers Stadium. But now, in the off season, members of the Steelers' "500 Club" preferred to lift in the basement of the Red Bull Inn in the Pittsburgh suburb of McMurray.

"There was an ambiance to the place," said defensive end John Banaszak.

It was an ambiance that had nothing to do with potted plants, art or music. It had to do with replicating a Spartan-type existence for an hour or two. The basement of the Red Bull Inn, now called Curinga's Restaurant after owner and powerlifter Lou Curinga, had that kind of soul. It's what attracted the 500-pound bench-pressers, a hard-core group consisting of Steve Furness, Mike Webster, Jon Kolb and Steve Courson. Others would drop in from time to time. They still do.

"When my son started lifting a few years ago," Banaszak said, "I took him down there instead of those yuppie places. You can't beat Curinga's."

Nor could you beat those who came out of Curinga's. Kolb won the "NFL Strongest Man" competition in 1978. Webster was second and Furness was fourth. Webster won in 1979, and in 1980 he beat Kolb in a showdown for the TV show *Strongest Man in Football*.

Furness had fallen behind his power-lifting teammates in 1979 since he was rehabilitating a broken leg suffered in the final two minutes of the Super Bowl. But Courson was gearing up for a big run, and he was doing so scientifically. In the off season of 1979, Courson was in the middle of his peak anabolic cycle during which he consumed approximately 56 ounces of steroids a week.

Courson came clean on the topic in 1985, but cast aspersions on the rest of his teammates by calling the Steelers "the steroid team of the '70s." He also accused Chuck Noll of having looked the other way, which was disputed by testimony during Courson's attempt to sue the NFL for higher benefits in 1997.

At the time of the suit, Courson needed a heart transplant and sought compensation from a league that he felt had led him into a life of steroid and alcohol abuse. Courson lost the suit and has since recovered.

Furness and Webster weren't as fortunate.

Furness died of a heart attack February 9, 2000, at the age of 49. Webster's heart stopped September 24, 2002, at the age of 50. And the question naturally arose: Were those two steroid abusers as well?

It couldn't be proven by doctors. In fact, doctors took a part in exonerating them. They warned those who were quick to jump to conclusions that Furness's family had a history of heart trouble. And doctors combed through Webster's medial records when his family applied to the NFL Pension Fund for disability. They couldn't find a link to steroids. Doctors did find that several concussions had damaged Webster's frontal lobe and his condition had progressively worsened. One doctor said Webster was "punch drunk."

"All I know is that Steve has admitted to steroids," said Banaszak. "When he made that blanket statement, well, I wasn't going to investigate it.

"It didn't make me mad. I know I didn't use steroids and I know that a lot of my teammates did not use them. No, I wasn't mad. Of course, I can't speak for everybody. I just know my guys. I know those guys. People want to talk about Webby, but you're going to get an argument from me because I knew him. Never saw it; didn't care to look for it. It's a non-issue."

In an *ESPN The Magazine* article from 2003 that probed the 1980 Strongest Man show, author Shaun Assael relayed a conversation between Webster and another participant, Terry Stieve.

Mike Webster's (52) massive arms and early death led to suspicions of steroid abuse, but doctors never found a link.

"Mike," Stieve says, leaning forward. "What are you up to? What are you on?"

"For the next five minutes," Stieve said, "I got the biggest lecture I've ever heard about the dangers of steroids. To this day, I don't believe Mike Webster touched them."

JACK SPLAT, PART II

Jack Lambert didn't take steroids. "Sure, I was temped to try them," he told the *Akron Beacon-Journal* in 1999. "There, right before me, was a way to gain the weight I couldn't put on no matter how much I ate. I just decided I wouldn't do it. I'd do my best and what happened, happened."

Lambert certainly didn't need them to play better. Nor did he need them to become enraged.

In the wee hours of May 4, Lambert became involved in another brawl, this one at the Happy Landing Lounge on Stanwix Street near Pittsburgh's Market Square. Newspapers reported only that someone had approached Lambert from behind and conked him on the head with a beer mug. A brawl erupted and police were dispatched.

No charges were filed, but at 3 a.m. Lambert was treated for facial cuts and abrasions at Divine Providence Hospital. He needed two stitches on his right ear.

It was the second known barroom brawl in 1979 for Lambert, and it began to worry the Steelers.

"He has to come to the realization that he has to exercise caution when he goes into places like that," said team president Dan Rooney. "It's like watching the cowboy movies on TV … the fastest gun around."

It's the same terminology sportswriter Vic Ketchman used 25 years later.

"A lot of those guys, especially Jack, if they went in the local watering holes, ran the risk of somebody recognizing them and looking to become the fastest gun in the west," Ketchman said. "The tough-guy types could expand their territory, and Lambert was the epitome of the tough-guy Steeler. If you kicked Ham's ass, you beat up a great player, but he didn't have the title Lambert had. Jack's reputation was similar to Joe Greene's, but Greene didn't go into those places."

Lambert couldn't stay out of them.

"I have two choices," he told the *Pittsburgh Press* at the time. "I can go out in public or I can stay home and live the life of a hermit, and I won't do that. Nobody can tell me how to live my life."

Lambert could find trouble anywhere. After a game in Denver, the Steelers returned to the airport and, while walking down the hallway with the team, Lambert was flagged down by a state trooper. The cop had recently pulled Lambert over for speeding but let him off with a warning. Now the trooper wanted payback in the form of Lambert's appearance at a party upstairs.

Since it was past 2 a.m., Lambert, even though he'd recognized the cop, cordially declined. The cop responded by calling Lambert an ungrateful prima donna and Lambert in turn jumped in the cop's face and began shouting.

"He was the most popular of all Steelers. Period," said Ketchman.

"In Pittsburgh, Lambert was the man. All of those tough millworkers, beer drinkers, all the real fans, identified with him. He was the guy they loved and whose attention they sought the most. So he couldn't go into a bar without someone targeting him. He couldn't walk through an airport without someone wanting his attention. It was a great life to live, but it brought with it demands and all of that tough-guy stuff.

"The fans wanted more than anything to identify with the Steelers, and Lambert was the embodiment of their image. When he walked into a bar, the whole franchise walked in. And if you took him out, you took out everybody on that team."

Colquitt in Car Accident

Less than a week after Jack Lambert's latest brawl made headline news, punter Craig Colquitt was charged with drunken driving after an auto accident in Knoxville, Tennessee.

Colquitt struck a tree and left a 21-year-old University of Tennessee student, Holly Bryant, with permanent brain damage.

Colquitt had a blood-alcohol level of 1.2 and in July was sued for $3 million for negligence by the woman's legal guardian, while Bryant remained in a coma.

Seventeen months later, Colquitt was cleared of the charges.

Colquitt testified he had two drinks at dinner before the accident. He estimated he was traveling between 40 and 50 miles per hour and that his tires locked as the car went into a curve in the road. Colquitt said he administered mouth-to-mouth resuscitation to Bryant and then drank from a whiskey bottle stashed in his car.

The arresting officer, Dan Stewart, testified Colquitt was so upset when the police arrived that he said, "If she dies, I'm going to kill myself." Stewart said he was so worried about Colquitt's condition that he secured his revolver inside the police car before moving Colquitt to the car.

A third-round draft pick in 1978, Colquitt was one of the first punters to require only two steps before kicking the ball. He led the NFL in net punting average (35.2) as a rookie. He played college football at Tennessee and was in Knoxville for classes at the time of the accident. Colquitt was recommended to the Steelers by former Pitt and Tennessee coach Johnny Majors.

J.T. THOMAS COMEBACK POSSIBLE

Prior to the 1978 season, the NFL changed its rules regarding bump-and-run coverage. No longer could defenders bump receivers more than five yards off the line of scrimmage. It was designed to put more offense into the game.

"You couldn't jam past five yards," said Mel Blount, "but you still had those five yards."

Blount, a six-foot-four cornerback with the Steelers, had used his size and strength to control receivers to that point, and he wouldn't admit to being affected by the rule change. But his style had been given a serious blow.

Blount also lost his partner, J.T. Thomas, before the 1978 season. The two played cornerback for the AFC in the Pro Bowl following the 1977 season, but Thomas sat out the 1978 season with a rare blood disease known as Boeck Sarcoid.

Although the Steelers drafted Ron Johnson in the first round of the 1978 draft, no rookie was going to make up for the absence of the underrated Thomas.

"J.T. Thomas was a perfect corner for cover-2," remembered Bud Carson, the Steelers' defensive coordinator and secondary coach up until 1978. "You can't just get a little piss-ant out there and ask him to play cover-2. Those receivers will run right over you. But J.T. was an outstanding corner. He's always been one of my favorites."

Carson left for the Los Angeles Rams after the 1977 season, and then safeties Glenn Edwards and Jimmy Allen were traded. Thomas, who'd played against his doctor's advice in 1975, took heed and sat out in 1978. The Steelers got by at cornerback that season with Blount and rookies Johnson and Larry Anderson. The latter was drafted in the fourth round because of his kick-returning skills. So it was with a sigh of relief that the Steelers welcomed Thomas back to mini-camp in the spring of 1979.

"He could really help us," defensive coordinator Woody Widenhofer told the *Pittsburgh Press*.

Of course, Chuck Noll wasn't as optimistic. "You never know what's going to happen," Noll said.

THE THUNDERING BULL

Chuck Noll once said of running back Sidney Thornton, "He has many problems and they are great." The statement was made near the end of Thornton's six-year career, but in 1979, his third pro season, Thornton was held in high regard.

"He had that wonderful word: potential," said Rocky Bleier, who was being pushed by Thornton for the Steelers' starting halfback job.

"They didn't call him the bull for nothing. He was solidly built, strong. When you were holding those bags in simulation blocks, it was like 'Geez.' And he ran strong."

But …

"But Sidney was his own worst enemy," Bleier said. "I think Sidney really wanted to do well. Sometimes you question whether he had the drive and maybe he'd say he did, and maybe he did, but it didn't seem to come out that way. Then there was understanding the plays and knowing where to run and who to block. That takes time. Plus, Sidney fumbled the ball. What happens is sometimes those things manifest themselves. You worry about them and they become a part of your playing habits."

It appeared Thornton was also worried about his job security when a newspaper in his hometown of Natchitoches, Louisiana, relayed a conversation Thornton had with Terry Bradshaw at a local football camp.

Sidney Thornton: They didn't call him The Bull for nothing.

Figuring Bradshaw "was tight with Noll," and knowing the Steelers had just drafted two running backs among their first three picks, Thornton asked Bradshaw about his status with the team.

"You're gone," Bradshaw cracked. "You'll be on the next plane to Minnesota as soon as they get it worked out."

That insecurity was the reason, Pittsburgh writers assumed, Thornton had "volunteered" to attend mini-camp that May. But Thornton resented the implication.

"Do you think I want to come?" Thornton asked Stellino of the *Post-Gazette*. "Don't think for a minute it was my idea. Is that in the paper? I hope you straighten this out."

Thornton explained he was lifting weights at the club's facility the previous week when Noll asked him if he wanted to come to mini-camp. That's when Thornton "volunteered."

So what did Thornton think of the draft?

"I don't pay the draft no attention," he told Stellino.

THE SWEET SCIENCE

Jack Lambert's predilection for settling disagreements with his fists was nothing new to the Steelers organization. In fact, the Chief and his brothers Dan and Vincent were prizefighters in the 1920s.

Dan, who became a priest, spent time, according to the 1973 book *About Three Bricks Shy Of A Load*, "protecting Chinese nuns from Communist troops with his fists." And Vincent was also known by his professional boxing name of Duke York.

As a young man one night in New York City, the Chief and his party became annoyed by an obnoxious drunk. Rooney befriended the man and bought him a few more drinks. Once the man was completely drunk, the Chief gave him a sound thrashing. Seated nearby was the governor of New York, Al Smith, who shook Rooney's hand and thanked him.

The players, of course, had a history of mixing it up in the streets long before Lambert came along. Linebacker Myron

Pottios, from the Pittsburgh mill-town suburb of Charleroi, was arrested in 1966 for fighting four policemen who'd been called to break up a brawl involving Pottios. He was traded the next day, but some of his brawling teammates remained.

"About five to 10 times a year, a guy would look at me and not be very impressed and start," former Steelers center Ray Mansfield told the *Post-Gazette*.

Mansfield told a story of accidentally bumping a patron standing next to him at a bar, not once but twice. After the second bump, the man pulled a gun on Mansfield, who simply turned his back.

"If he was going to shoot me, it would have to be in the back," Mansfield said.

Former linebacker Andy Russell saw a man thrown through a picture window by a 1960s-era Steelers offensive tackle. And defensive tackle Ernie Stautner and fullback Tom Tracy were known as bodyguards for quarterback Bobby Layne when he was out drinking.

No charges were filed in Lambert's most recent brawl. Rumors still circulate that his opponent that early morning was a mobster who later put out a contract, or "a hit", on the Achilles' tendon of the revenge-minded Lambert.

"That's not true," said a witness. "They left it all in the bar that night."

The witness said the brawl was actually started by Lambert, who "was a pain in the ass. He used to drink at The Foggy Bottom in West Mifflin all the time, and he was a pain in the ass there, too."

Scare in the Air

New York Yankees catcher Thurman Munson died August 2, 1979 after his airplane crashed while he was practicing a landing. Chuck Noll was talking it over with reporters when he revealed that his own private plane began spraying oil over Elkins, West Virginia, during a flight in June.

Noll piloted his wife, Marianne, son Chris and a few friends aboard his Beechcraft on a return trip from Hilton Head, S.C. The pressure began to drop so Noll turned off the bad engine and "feathered the prop" into Allegheny County Airport. Noll called the incident routine.

"It was one of those emergency situations that makes flying interesting," he said.

Noll was asked if the incident, coupled with Munson's death, might cause him to stop flying.

"Absolutely not," he said. "Nothing is sure in this life, and you can't take the risks out of it. If you did, the enjoyment could be gone, too."

Training Camp Closing In

John Banaszak survived the summer of '79—barely. He and right guard Gerry Mullins, back-up quarterback Cliff Stoudt and back-up safety Ray Oldham went to Puerto Rico as part of a Steelers promotion and made their way to a golf course. A few of them were lucky to come back after surviving an accident in their golf cart.

Banaszak was driving the cart with Oldham riding along. They began speeding down a hill toward a lake. Banaszak swerved left and a wheel caught a rut in the ground and snapped the cart wheel back to the right. It began heading over a 12-foot drop into the middle of the lake, which was actually a knee-deep swamp. Oldham jumped out and the cart flipped and landed on Banaszak, a 244-pound defensive end.

"The thing landed, boom, right on the roof and just smashed," Banaszak said. "I was lying underneath this thing on the floorboard, saying, 'Wow, that was quite a ride.' I was making sure I could move my legs and arms."

Oldham began screaming, "Banny, Banny, are you all right?"

Banaszak didn't say anything initially, and Oldham's shouts became louder. Banaszak finally responded and Oldham helped lift the cart off Banaszak, who slithered out.

On the fairway, Stoudt had heard the shouting, but couldn't see anything. He thought it was a prank.

"We climbed out of this swamp and we had all this black, swamp mud all over us, and there was gasoline leaking on me," Banaszak said. "I thought I was going to start on fire."

Stoudt was aghast and helped his teammates retrieve the clubs, money and jewelry scattered throughout the swamp.

"We got everything," Banaszak said. "The strange thing was, in my flight down, I missed a 24-inch culvert pipe by a few feet. I think that might've caused a little more damage."

As it was, Banaszak was fine for the start of training camp.

And the golf game?

"We called for another cart, filled out a damage report and finished the round."

CHAPTER IV

TRAINING CAMP:
HELL WITH THE LID
NAILED SHUT

"I'm sure Chuck knows we didn't walk around St. Vincent with halos over our heads."

—Defensive end John Banaszak

AT THE FOOT OF THE
LAUREL MOUNTAINS

St. Vincent College is nestled in the foothills of the Laurel Mountains in Latrobe, home of the first professional football game in 1895.

And nestled among the nestled is a plot of land big enough to hold three football fields. It's surrounded by three hills that hold the heat and humidity. It's not blown easily up over those Laurel Mountains.

"If you can see the peaks of those mountains during morning practice," running backs coach Dick Hoak likes to say, "the heat in the afternoon will be manageable. But if you can't see those peaks in the morning, look out."

On most steamy August mornings, you won't see those peaks. The reporters and fans who simply stand and wither and watch the afternoon practices understand Hoak's point. The players just don't allow themselves to think about the mugginess, or the heat index, which routinely flirts with 100 degrees. On the particularly tough days, no one's surprised at a reading of 110 degrees.

Tom Moore was a 40-year-old wide receivers coach in 1979. That summer he was preparing for his third season in the league after leaving the University of Minnesota for the Steelers along with his quarterback, Tony Dungy. Moore fondly remembers the work ethic of his Hall of Fame pupils with the Steelers, Lynn Swann and John Stallworth, but couldn't come up with specific examples.

"Back in my first year," Moore said, "training camps were nine weeks long, so just their consistency throughout.

"I mean, you've been in Latrobe. It's not real cool up there."

Training camp didn't last nine weeks in 1979, but the six weeks the Steelers spent at St. Vincent in 1979 was nearly twice that of training camps a quarter-century later.

"Now," groused L.C. Greenwood, the Steelers' premier pass rusher of the '70s, "training camp is like a vacation to the islands somewhere."

Then Greenwood lowered his voice and leaned in as if were about to break a sacred trust.

"Personally," he said, "I liked training camp."

The players never admitted it then, and with good reason, but 25 years later, Greenwood longs for the structure, the discipline, of training camp.

"You go there to work, to condition yourself for the season, to mentally prepare yourself and physically prepare yourself to play the game," he said. "And you get away from all the other distractions like the families, the reasons why you can't get up in the morning and go work out. You get away from all that. You go there, you get up in the morning, have breakfast, go work out, practice. It's a constant diet of football.

"I think that's important in any sport. It's important the player get the opportunity to get away from the problems, situations that he has to deal with, and get there and his mind is strictly on conditioning the body because they run you till you can't run no more. They practice you till you just can't practice anymore.

"I really liked camp. It gave me a chance to really work."

The Art of Starting Over

Twice in his essay in *Game Plans For Success*, Chuck Noll asks: Is it harder to take a team to the top or to stay on top?

He didn't have an answer because Noll started over every year. While the Steelers had successfully defended a title once before, the experience of 1975 did them little good as they prepared for 1979—at least in Noll's eyes.

"We expect to have our problems," he said at his precamp press conference. "Football teams usually do."

On the eve of camp, the Steelers learned they would lose Ray Pinney until at least late August. The fourth-year pro had replaced an injured Larry Brown at right tackle in 1978 and played well against Ed "Too Tall" Jones in the Super Bowl. But Pinney experienced complications from an appendectomy and would miss camp, as would rookie wide receiver Calvin Sweeney, who missed 1979 with a bum foot.

Position battles loomed for veteran starters on each side of the ball. At halfback, Sidney Thornton entered camp as a threat to Rocky Bleier. At right defensive end, John Banaszak was listed ahead of Dwight White on the depth chart.

The biggest question mark was age. Twelve of 24 returning starters would be at least 30 years old on opening day, but Noll had an answer at the ready: "We're not interested in any kind of transfusions."

The secondary was also a question mark. J.T. Thomas was returning from a year off due to a blood disorder. Would he be ready to step in if, say, 31-year-old cornerback Mel Blount or 30-year-old free safety Mike Wagner couldn't? Thomas would become a valuable swing substitute in the secondary if healthy.

There were other questions: Was it time for 1977 No. 1 draft pick Robin Cole to supplant Loren Toews at right outside linebacker? Would one of the youngsters backing up the offensive line—Steve Courson, Thom Dornbrook, Ted Peterson—steal a job from, say, 35-year-old Sam Davis? Were Gary Dunn and Tom Beasley ready to steal a job on the defensive line?

"Beasley showed a lot of great things in practice," Noll told reporters. "He was practicing real well the week before

Chuck Noll didn't believe in picking up where the team had left off. He started over every training camp.

the Super Bowl. If he hadn't turned his ankle, I'd have played him."

Remember, this was a team which, according to Noll, hadn't peaked yet.

"I hope I can say that after this season," he said.

THE OKLAHOMA DRILL

In 1974, while the veterans held out of training camp as part of a league-wide strike, the Steelers' prized rookies took center stage. And on the first day, Chuck Noll matched linebacker Jack Lambert with center Mike Webster, who outweighed Lambert by nearly 50 pounds.

The mismatch was obvious to Musick of the *Post-Gazette*.

"Where did you find this stiff Lambert at?" he asked personnel boss Art Rooney, Jr.

Even though Webster usually had his way with Lambert, it became the most anticipated match-up of the most anticipated drill throughout—and even beyond—the Steelers' championship years.

The Oklahoma drill pitted an offensive lineman against a defender, between a pair of blocking dummies, as a back looked for running room somewhere within three feet of terrain. This "nutcracker," as some of the coaches called it, was done on the first day of training camp in order to set a tone. By 1979, the crowds at St. Vincent College were as large as 10,000 for the Oklahoma drill.

"It's not exactly a fair drill," said defensive tackle Gary Dunn. "You had two dummies instead of a player next to you so in a stalemate the running back could slide off the side of the dummy. There wasn't anybody else to tackle him. It's nothing like a game condition. And sometimes the running backs wouldn't run in the lanes because they knew you were going to knock the shit out of them, especially Franco.

"It was more symbolic than anything, but it got the hitting going."

It didn't take much for Lambert. He broke into a fight with Thom Dornbrook during his first Oklahoma match-up that year, but everyone awaited his showdown with Webster. The two had fought during the 1974 match-up and entertained fans and players for years.

"Webby was a lot bigger than Jack," Dunn said. "But it was funny because Jack would yell at him and scream at him and it would be pretty comical. Jack would scream at Mike and Mike would smile because he knew that was Jack being Jack."

UNDER THE BIG TOP

Chuck Noll's training camps were known for physical contact, timed 350-yard runs and weightlifting under and around the on-field tent, after practice, in "the heat of the day."

"Chuck was big on the power lifts, like the power cleans," said John Banaszak, who could hang with the best of the team's powerlifters.

L.C. Greenwood was a weightlifting legend in his own right. He was known to walk into a weight room, set his lit cigarette to the side, bench 135 pounds 10 times, pick his cigarette back up and walk out. Another workout in the books.

"A hundred thirty-five, oh, no," Banaszak said. "That was way too much weight for him. No, no, no. Way too much. I remember they put 135 pounds on this bar and L.C. tried to do this power clean. He was way off balance and one of the weights fell off the other side and he'd snap it back on the other side and there were weights flying everywhere, bars flying everywhere. Chuck's running out of the way 'cause he don't want to get hurt. And he told L.C., 'Get out of here before you hurt me or yourself.'

"It was hilarious, but nobody could block L.C. Greenwood."

"I'd lift pretty much to rehabilitate," said Greenwood. "I'd go in the weight room on the certain days and do what Chuck wanted me to do. I was into stretching and running. On the Saturdays before games, I'd run two, three miles around the track while Chuck was working with the special teams. I just thought if I was in better physical condition to run than I had a better chance to wear the guy down in front of me. If you're quick enough, you're strong enough."

Not once in his 13 years in the NFL did Greenwood leave a game because he was tired.

"There's more than one way to play the game," said Banaszak. "Everybody tries to be bigger, faster, stronger and what you lose in trying to accomplish that is natural ability. That's what he had. He was blessed with very long arms, blessed with the ability to reduce his body. He got skinny, man."

So what exactly was it like lifting under the big top after practice?

"The serious, serious weightlifters would go up inside the gym and lift inside the weight room," Banaszak said. "The casual weightlifters would go in the tent and do a couple of sets because Chuck was there, and then head to The 19th Hole."

JACK AND THE RATTLESNAKE

Chuck Noll had reminded reporters to keep an eye on Tom Beasley, but Jack Lambert didn't need reminding. He had his eye on Beasley the moment the back-up defensive tackle and his friend, a competitive rattlesnake hunter, showed up at training camp with a rattlesnake in a cage.

"Hey, Beas," Lambert called as the rest of the Steelers milled past the cage after practice. "Whatever you do, keep that snake away from me. I don't want to have anything to do with that snake."

Beasley nodded. He was aware snakes were Lambert's one great fear.

The players left the field, showered, ate and hit the bars that night. Lambert went, too, and was one of the stragglers as he returned to his room at St. Bonaventure Hall just before the 11 o'clock curfew.

Once in his room, Lambert saw the rattlesnake cage with the gate swung open, but no rattlesnake.

"I heard this screaming down the hall," said Gary Dunn. "It was Jack and he was yelling, 'Beasley, that's attempted murder! Attempted murder, dammit!' And then he started yelling for Chuck. 'Chuck, get out here! Attempted murder! Beasley's trying to kill me! He put a rattlesnake in my room!'"

The rest of the players popped out of their rooms in varying stage of undress. Chuck Noll poked his head out of his room.

"Jack, what's your problem?"

"Coach," Lambert said. "Beasley's trying to kill me. He put a rattlesnake in my room."

Noll walked upstairs to the room with Lambert, who was one of the few players without a roommate. They walked in and Noll, upon seeing the open cage, said, "Now are you sure you saw the snake actually in this cage? In this room?"

"Hey, Chuck," Lambert said. "THAT snake was in THAT cage and THAT snake is in THIS room right now."

With that, Noll jumped back into the hallway.

"Jack," Noll said, "Get out of the room right now, close the door and leave it there. Go sleep somewhere else."

The players who were in on the prank went downstairs, had a good laugh and told Lambert the snake's owner had set up the gag and taken the snake home. A fuming Lambert stepped outside to smoke a cigarette.

"Meanwhile," Dunn said, "Beas puts a rubber snake under his pillow. So after all this commotion, Jack finally goes to bed, gets into bed, pulls down the covers, reaches his hand under the pillow and hits this rubber snake. He went through the roof and started hollering again, 'Beasley! It's murder! It's murder.'"

MEAN JOE AND TRADITION

The Steelers of the Ray Mansfield–Bruce Van Dyke era of the late 1960s and early 1970s made the postpractice, predinner shuttle to The 19th Hole a daily ritual.

The tradition is a thing of the past, but in 1979 the players still hit "The Hole" in the afternoon, and at night hit either The Intermission, Halula's, Bobby Dale's, even Pete's if they didn't mind bumping into the coaching staff.

"I'm sure Chuck knows we didn't walk around St. Vincent with halos over our heads," said John Banaszak.

As the returning veterans plotted new escapades at one end of the practice field during Photo Day '79, Joe Greene held his annual pre-season talk with reporters at the other end. Soon to turn 33, Greene had plenty of nuggets.

On the Steelers resuming their place atop the NFL:

Terry Bradshaw (12) lent whimsy and a degree of folksiness to the proceedings at training camp, while Mean Joe Greene (75) was the resident philosopher.

"I missed it and I think some other guys did, too," Greene said. "And I think we wear the crown pretty damn well."

On what it took:

"There are probably four or five teams that have the talent we have, but leadership and philosophy are the keys."

On his future plans:

"That stuff about going out on top is bull. We have a good shot at being very successful again this year. The only thing that can keep us from losing it is injury."

On the difference between now and 1976, their previous title defense which ultimately failed:

"I think our feet were on the ground then. It was just a happening. Some days the sun shines and some days it rains. When you play well, you got to come down sometime. It's not going to get us any crowns looking back."

"Mean Joe" Greene was championed by reporters during his playing days as one who didn't say much, but what he said mattered.

"I think that came about by being in Chuck's environment and how he communicated to the team, how he communicated to the fans, how he communicated to the press, and that was probably the best way to do it, emulate him in some form," Greene said 25 years later.

"Chuck as a coach and a person, he was very solid. He didn't waver. 'If you do these things you'll get these results,' he'd say, and you tended to believe him."

SWANN V. SAN FRANCISCO

On January 28, 1974 three people were murdered and two others wounded—all white—by a group of black Muslims known as the Zebra Killers. They were eventually convicted of killing 12 white people in the San Francisco area in a period of weeks.

On January 31, 1974 the Bay Area's Lynn Swann was drafted in the first round by the Steelers. That night, he and two brothers—Calvin Swann, a social worker, and Dr. Brian Swann, a Palo Alto dentist—and cousin Michael Henderson headed out to a restaurant to celebrate.

The car was pulled over by police, who were operating under orders to randomly stop and search small groups of black males.

Swann and his party were cited for running a red light.

"A bad call," said Lynn, who just wanted to sign the ticket and move on. But according to testimony, one of the cops called them "black monkeys" and "black aborigines."

After Brian, the driver, presented his license, he was also cited for "presenting a mutilated driver's license." At that point, Calvin reacted angrily and a scuffle broke out. The group was arrested on charges ranging from disturbing the peace to assault and battery. They were eventually cleared of all charges, but not before being handcuffed and taken to the police station.

There, the group walked a gauntlet of 10 to 15 cops to cross the parking lot. Lynn Swann testified he was beaten in the knee with a nightstick and kicked in the groin several times. Inside the station, a desk officer with a nightstick smashed the watch he was given for being named the PAC Eight MVP.

"Aw, look, your watch is broken," the cop said.

"Oh, you're a football player," said another. "You've had worse beatings than this."

As a result, the four men sued the City and County of San Francisco for $2 million.

After three continuances, the statutes of limitations had run out but were extended. Swann's lawyer, Michael Keady, then asked for another delay on May 21, 1979.

"I think Swann did it to stay out of training camp," City Attorney Kevin O'Donnell told the judge.

"They just want him to look bad in the media," Keady said. "But Lynn wanted the last delay because he was getting married."

Sure enough, one of Pittsburgh's most proudly eligible bachelors had been reeled in. But because of the trial, Swann would be grounded in San Francisco for much of training camp.

ROOKIE LEADS STEELERS IN OPENER

Only one rookie had a realistic chance of cracking the Steelers' starting lineup in 1979, and kicker Matt Bahr increased those chances by making all three of his field-goal attempts in a 15-7 win on the road against the Buffalo Bills in the preseason opener.

At the time, Bahr wasn't too happy with his performance. He'd missed an extra point and had placed only one of six kickoffs inside the Buffalo 5-yard line. One kick was re-done because it went out of bounds.

Of his field goals, a 39-yarder bounced off an upright, and the field goal which put the Steelers ahead with 1:12 left, a 25-yarder, came within inches of an upright. Bahr's longest field goal, a 41-yarder, was perfect.

One newspaperman, citing the three for three, predicted it would become a memorable performance for the rookie, but Bahr barely remembered it 25 years later.

"What I remember most about training camp actually was the German nuns and the good food," he said. "Apparently, a lot of those sisters had escaped Nazi Germany and were still there at St. Vincent in the late '70s."

Bahr recalled incumbent kicker Roy Gerela as "an acquaintance." Bahr was also impressed by the devotion of the fans, who thickly lined the walks to and from the practice field.

"I also remember that, without fanfare, Jack Lambert would sign autographs until there were none left to sign. He would miss lunch, even his rest time, and just sign all the way through until he had to get ready for the next practice. I don't know how many times he did that, but I thought it showed a lot of character."

Did Bahr remember being intimidated by his larger-than-life teammates?

"Mel Blount said something interesting to me many years later," Bahr recalled. "It appeared to me that he and Roy Gerela were good friends. When Roy got cut, I felt that by default I had become the focus of Mel's ire. But it wasn't the case. He said it was quite the opposite. He said, 'You were our teammate.' And that goes back to the classiness of all those superstars, all those Hall of Famers. Everyone is a teammate and they're pulling for you to succeed, not necessarily to play to their level, the superstars' level, but to play to the best of your ability.

"At the time, I don't think I realized that, but when you look back at how you were treated, absolutely, I was one of their teammates."

CAMP BATTLES

Cornerback J.T. Thomas answered one big question with his solid performance in Buffalo. The questions about the starting jobs at the two open positions were also being answered.

Injuries to Rocky Bleier and first-round pick Greg Hawthorne left the halfback job to Sidney Thornton by default. Bleier sprained his knee against the Bills while Hawthorne had pulled a hamstring on the first day of camp.

The right defensive end job, split between Dwight White and John Banaszak in 1978, went to White in the opener after he'd won a coach's coin flip. But it was Banaszak who played better. Banaszak had two sacks and forced a fumble that Gary Dunn returned for a touchdown. White made one tackle, but was undeterred.

"I don't think I lost a damn thing," White said at the time. "Chuck Noll's theory is that football is a test of the whole man. I'm up to that test."

White reminded reporters of Super Bowl IX and how he'd spent the previous week in a hospital bed, lost 18 pounds and wasn't supposed to play.

Noll told doctors the day of that Super Bowl: "We'll let him on the field for warmups, and then when he keels over we'll drag him off."

Of course, White was a big reason the Steelers held the Minnesota Vikings to 119 yards, a Super Bowl record low to this day, in a 16-6 Steelers win.

Defensive line coach George Perles said of White's performance: "He played like a guy going into a burning house after his family."

With those memories still fresh, the Steelers kept the 30-year-old White in the hunt with Banaszak for the starting job, and ahead of hotshot rookie Dwaine Board for a roster spot.

"They were ready to bury me in New Orleans," White said at the '79 training camp. "I wasn't ready to die. All sickness ain't death."

SWANN V. NOLL

Lynn Swann left the trial before its completion in order to minimize the damage he'd done to his relationship with Chuck Noll.

Prior to the first day, Swann asked Noll for permission to miss time in camp, but Noll refused.

"He asked about his status," Noll told reporters two weeks into camp, "and I told him that as far as I'm concerned he has retired."

So Swann did. It caused a furor for a few days until Swann sent official notice to reporters, through the Steelers, that he would return as soon as possible.

On August 10, after dodging 200 fans and a battery of media at the airport, Swann reported to St. Vincent College to end his 20-day "retirement."

As expected, he showed signs of rust during his first practice.

"It'll be awhile before Lynn Swann is back," Noll said. "Right now, he's just another guy named Lynn."

And that was fine with his teammates, since Swann was one of the heartiest practical jokers of the group.

"He'd put talcum powder in people's helmets, water in the shoulder pads, tape guys up," said Matt Bahr. "Taping guys up was one of the big things at camp."

So Swann went right back to work. He and his fellow wide receivers snared Rocky Bleier one day and taped him to the crossbar of the goal post, upside down, in the form of a cocoon.

"It was a colder day and I made the mistake of cutting him down," Bahr said. "You're not supposed to do that, so the receivers jumped me later to tape me up and I fought back tooth and nail."

As Bahr weakened, Swann and company taped his ankles together. Bahr called out to Franco Harris and Jack Ham, fellow Penn Staters, and they began pulling receivers off the rookie kicker.

"The offensive linemen didn't want Franco to get hurt, so they came over to help and I escaped," Bahr said. "But the receivers told the offensive linemen later that I'd cut Rocky down, which is a no-no. So one of the offensive linemen came up behind me one day and grabbed me by both wrists, and I couldn't move a muscle. I called out for my Penn State help, but Franco and Hammer saw it was the offensive linemen and they shook me off."

Bahr ended up taped to Noll's desk, which broke during Bahr's subsequent struggle to escape. Noll fixed the desk, but never traced the damage back to some guy named Lynn.

Lynn Swann was forced to retire from football for three weeks during the 1979 training camp. He successfully sued the city of San Francisco for police brutality.

Get the Broom Out

The Steelers swept the New York teams in the second and third preseason games. The 10-3 win over the Giants may have been the Steelers' dullest win of the 1970s. If it wasn't for Greg Hawthorne's 29-yard reception on his first live play in 10 months, perhaps even Chuck Noll would've dozed off.

In a 27-14 win over the Jets, the offense finally showed signs of life and Roy Gerela made a bid to save his job by kicking a pair of 48-yard field goals.

Gerela found out four days later his effort fell short. He was cut by Noll, who opted to keep rookie Matt Bahr instead of the 31-year-old Gerela. His departure left the Steelers with 22 players from their first Super Bowl team.

Popular Dungy Traded

On the day Tony Dungy was traded to the San Francisco 49ers for a 10th-round draft pick, Terry Bradshaw, Franco Harris, Lynn Swann and Joe Greene held a going-away party for him in Greene's room.

If you're counting, that's four Hall of Famers for one third-year reserve.

The *Post-Gazette* reported the parting shots and prophesies: "Don't you have to turn in your ring?" asked Bradshaw.

"Don't let the coach out there know you're smarter than he is," said Swann.

"You'll be a leader out there," said Greene.

Dungy left the Steelers after only two seasons as a reserve safety, but he'd intercepted nine passes and inhaled a defensive system which had been completely foreign to him.

"I didn't know anything about defensive football because I was an offensive player from elementary school all the way through college," Dungy said 25 years later. "In two years I learned pretty much my whole philosophy of defensive football. By the time I left there as a player, I understood the game of football. That's something Coach Noll worked on."

Dungy led the Steelers in interceptions the previous season with six, but hardly played in three 1979 preseason games. He saw the writing on the wall when the Steelers began using cornerback J.T. Thomas at safety.

"We had a great year in '78 and had just about everybody back, so you felt they were going to have a good year again and I was looking forward to being a part of that," said Dungy, who's now the head coach of the Indianapolis Colts. "But that's, again, a lesson I tell the guys on my team now. Strike while the iron's hot. Don't say, 'Hey, we've got two years or three years or four years.' The team may, but as an individual you may not. That's a lesson I learned."

As the 1979 season went on, Dungy called his ex-teammates every week. He missed the vibe of a winning team. The 49ers finished 2-14.

"I knew when I left the odds were great they were going to win another championship," he said.

Dungy was surprised to learn later that his parents had received a heartfelt letter from Art Rooney, Sr.

"That's the Steeler way of doing things," Dungy said. "I wasn't even a draft choice. I was there two years and was a role player. But he wrote my mom and dad a letter just saying how he enjoyed me being on the team and enjoyed meeting them. It's something my mom always kept with her.

"Again, I've taken that part with me, that there's a classy way to do things and the players are more than just hired soldiers. That's the way Coach Noll was; that's the way Mr. Rooney was.

"When I came back to coach, Marianne Noll told me I was always one of Chuck's favorite guys because of the way I worked at it and the way I studied. I never would've known that if she hadn't told me because he just treated everybody the same way. He took an interest in everybody."

THE COOLING BOARD

Chuck Noll took an interest in rookie defensive end Dwaine Board. So did assistant head coach George Perles. So did scout Bill Nunn. But they couldn't save Board from taking it in the neck on the Steelers' final round of cuts.

"Really," said Nunn, "we did try to do everything we could to get him hurt."

The Steelers couldn't find a way to stash Board on injured reserve, then they couldn't trade him, even for a conditional 12th-round pick, because teams knew the Steelers would keep Dwight White instead. And so they cut Board.

"I was really pissed off about that," said Nunn, who, in his role as camp Turk, informed Board of the decision.

"I knew he'd be picked up and play somewhere else, and I told him that," Nunn said. "When they ended up in the Super Bowl three years later, he was quoted in the paper saying 'I wasn't worried because Bill Nunn said I could play.' That was in our paper and I said, 'Oh, Jesus.'"

Board was picked up by the San Francisco 49ers the next day and started 16 games at defensive end as a rookie. He spent 10 years in the league, won two Super Bowl rings and is officially credited with 45 sacks, even though the league didn't begin tracking the statistic until 1982.

"Board could've made the team," Nunn said.

Couldn't get him hurt, huh?

"We don't tell a player that," Nunn said with a laugh. "But we had certain drills. It just didn't happen."

PLANT THAT PILL AND LET IT RAIN

When rookie cornerback Dwayne Woodruff reported to training camp, a coach told him the Steelers had cut only one player from the University of Louisville—Johnny Unitas. So Woodruff went into the final round of cuts figuring he at least had karma on his side.

Veteran left tackle Jon Kolb, 32, wasn't sure. According to the *Pittsburgh Press*, Kolb was told by a ballboy that Chuck Noll

The Steelers' popularity peaked in Latrobe in the late 1970s. Five-figure crowds were common at St. Vincent College. Here, Terry Bradshaw accommodates some of those fans.

wanted to see him. Kolb thought he was being cut. He even wiped away a tear before stepping into Noll's office. That's where Noll showed Kolb a photo of a pileated woodpecker taken on a recent trip to the Everglades.

"Being a farm boy, I thought you might be able to appreciate these," Noll said.

Kolb's appreciation had never been greater.

But rookies Dwaine Board, Tom Graves, Larry Douglas, and veterans Ray Oldham and Jack Deloplaine weren't as fortunate. They were the final cuts on August 27.

Oldham, a reserve safety, played one year for the Steelers. They'd picked him up from the Baltimore Colts' scrap heap early in 1978 after rookie Randy Reutershan was in a car wreck.

Oldham played well in the Steelers' final preseason game, a 16-14 loss at Dallas. He played the entire second half in place of a limping J.T. Thomas, and drew praise for his effort. Then he was cut.

Deloplaine was second to Franco Harris in rushing that preseason but averaged only 2.3 yards a carry. Trying to make it to his fourth season with the Steelers, Deloplaine lost his job to free agent rookie running back Anthony Anderson, a better special teams player.

A potential problem cropped up when tackle Ray Pinney had to be placed on injured reserve and was lost for the season. Pinney returned to training camp in the middle of August, practiced while remaining out of contact drills for four days, but his stomach hadn't completely healed. The Steelers tried to put him on the physically unable to perform list, but the league didn't allow it since Pinney had practiced.

Larry Brown, the other right tackle, injured his groin in the final preseason game. He was expected to miss two to three weeks.

"We have to bring somebody in," moaned offensive line coach Rollie Dotsch, but the Steelers went with the eight offensive linemen on their roster. Steve Courson and Thom Dornbrook were back-up guards; Ted Peterson was the only back-up tackle. Right guard Gerry Mullins could play right tackle in a pinch.

Since the Steelers didn't pick up another tackle, they entered the season with a roster comprised of 45 homegrown and purebred players.

CHAPTER V

STRUGGLING EARLY:
A GLADIATOR'S GUIDE TO DEFENDING AN NFL TITLE

"Our physical abilities may have started to decline, but the will to win and the heart of some of these players was amazing to me."

—Free safety Mike Wagner

TAKING AIM AT HISTORY

Before Green Bay Packers middle linebacker Ray Nitschke died in 1998, he'd run into Steelers outside linebacker Jack Ham of the Pittsburgh Steelers at various functions. Not surprisingly, the two Hall of Famers talked about their respective glory days.

"What a quality guy," Ham remembered. "But I would always kid him, 'You guys couldn't even touch us.'"

In season, the Steelers' main rivals were the Houston Oilers, Oakland Raiders and Dallas Cowboys, but in terms of the big picture and what their legacy would be, the Steelers' rival at the dawn of the 1979 season was Nitschke's Packers.

Jack Lambert had brawled in the name of that rivalry one spring night. Chuck Noll wouldn't even allow his team to enjoy its third Super Bowl victory because of that chase for immortality.

The Packers won five NFL championships in seven years; the Steelers at that point had won three in five. Officially, the Steelers had won one more Super Bowl than the Packers, but a mere technicality wouldn't fool historians since both dynasties existed in the modern era of the game.

No, the Steelers would need to win one more NFL championship to be put on the same pedestal with the Packers, to even make the argument viable.

Could they win one more? Joe Greene knew the team was getting old. He knew he wasn't the same player he'd been in, say, 1975. But from the safety of 25 years removed, yes, Greene believed, the Steelers were capable of winning at least another title.

"I never put any doubts in my mind about what we were trying to get done because you never know, you're confident," Greene said. "When I start off by saying we were a little long in the tooth, that's probably said in hindsight, too. I wasn't thinking that at the time, but ultimately that's what happens. Teams get old."

"To be very candid with you, we had to hang on to win it," said Ham. "We were kind of smart enough to know that defensively we weren't anywhere near as dominant as we were in our previous Super Bowl years."

Did Ham know, in 1979, the end was near?

"Oh, yeah," he said. "I think we realized we had a group that hung together for a five-, six-, seven-year run, and I don't think tape will lie. I think we were smart enough, at least I was, and I'm sure the rest of the guys were as well, that any chance of going any further than that would have to be done with mirrors. Yeah, I think we realized it."

Was there then a sense of urgency?

"Oh I think so. The fourth one kind of put us in rarified air, so yeah it was important and I think we all realized that, too. You don't realize it at the beginning when you win your first one or first two, but all of the sudden you realize you have a pretty good streak going and it would be a good way to cap it off. We didn't even come close the next year. We didn't even make the playoffs."

So with the start of the 1979 season one week away, Noll was reminded once again of his proclamation following Super Bowl XIII: "I don't think we've peaked yet."

Now, he was cornered.

"I like being in a corner," Noll told reporters. "That way they can't get you from behind."

THE CHOBEE PARTY

With the roster set, Jack Lambert hosted his annual Chobee Party, named in honor of former defensive back Glenn Edwards.

"He was from Lake Okeechobee, the swamps," said Rocky Bleier. "You couldn't understand a thing Glenn said, and it would drive people nuts, Lambert specifically. So they started calling each other Chobees."

Lambert would host the preseason party at his home in Fox Chapel, and attendance was mandatory for all new line-backers and defensive backs. This was the group that would meet throughout the season for meetings and film review, so what better way to become acquainted?

"We'd give the new guys a hard time for awhile," said Mike Wagner. "But when the evening was over they all knew who we all were and how goofy or silly we all were. They also knew that we cared about them, and they knew the lay of the land. There were no holds barred. I think of all the things Jack did, that was one of the best."

Typically, as the season went on, the Chobees collected fines from each other for mistakes, and near the end of the season they'd use the money to party on the town.

"Jack loved the Chobee Party," said Bleier. "All Lambert would drink was Michelob, and he'd drink—and be fine, not punch drunk—maybe 10, 12, 15, and he was fine. Now, he said of some of his, um, brothers on the team: 'The problem is they don't know how to drink.' Well, they'd come in and have a mixed drink, then they'd go to a beer, then a glass of wine, then maybe a brandy. And so before dinner was over, a lot of them just passed out in their plate. Then Jack would take them out afterwards.

"Some guys never got home and they'd come to practice the next morning and Jack would always be there early. Jack would be at his locker with a cup of coffee, smoking a ciga-rette, waiting for the parade to come in. He just took extreme pleasure from guys coming in with their suits that they had on the night before, the same clothes, wrinkled, some had puke all over them. He just took extreme pleasure in that. You've got to be a complex guy to mastermind that kind of thing."

Rust Never Sleeps

In his book *A Steeler Odyssey*, Andy Russell wrote, "Joe Greene was unquestionably the NFL's best player in the seventies. No player had a greater impact or did more for his team."

On his first day of training camp in 1969, Greene tore into the sports editor of the *Pittsburgh Press* for criticizing his hold-out. Greene feared Pat Livingston about as much as he feared Dick Butkus, which is to say he didn't fear anyone.

After Butkus had flattened L.C. Greenwood on special teams near the Steelers sideline during the 1969 season, Greene charged Butkus, grabbed him by the shoulder pads with one hand and cocked his other arm back, poised to bludgeon Butkus with his helmet. Butkus freed himself and trotted across the field to his own sideline. Russell later asked Butkus why he'd backed down.

"I was having too much fun destroying your offense to get kicked out of that game—for fighting with that wildman rookie of yours," Butkus said.

Greene was the NFL's defensive rookie of the year in 1969 and defensive player of the year in both 1972 and 1974.

Frustrated by all of the double- and triple-team blocking he had been facing, Greene began lining his body at a sharp angle between the center and guard. He did this at the start of the 1974 playoffs and the Steelers allowed 146 rushing yards in three post-season games. In the Super Bowl, the Steelers allowed 17 rushing yards to the Minnesota Vikings. Greene also intercepted a pass and recovered a fumble.

"Joe Greene is the best I ever saw," Steelers defensive coordinator Bud Carson said after Super Bowl IX. "I just didn't think he could be any better, only he was."

Greene's career may have peaked in that game. In 1975, he slipped while warming up for a game and pinched a nerve in his neck. He saw limited action in the AFC Championship Game and Super Bowl X. The problems associated with the injury lingered into 1979.

"Yeah, I was a different player," Greene said 25 years later. "I probably wasn't—if I ever was an athletic person—but I probably wasn't quite as agile as I had been before. I played a different style of game. I only participated in one Super Bowl when I was healthy. Maybe healthy isn't the right word, but when I didn't have the neck injury."

Greene was named to his ninth Pro Bowl after the 1979 season. He eventually was named to a 10th before retiring after the 1981 season. Despite the injuries, Greene played in 181 out of a possible 190 games and was inducted into the Hall of Fame in 1987.

OVERCOMING INJURIES

The loss of right tackle Ray Pinney for the season was exacerbated by Larry Brown's groin injury in the final preseason game. Brown would miss the opener on Monday night at Foxboro against New England, as would right guard Gerry Mullins, who was scratched with an elbow injury. They were replaced by Ted Peterson at tackle and Steve Courson at guard.

Rocky Bleier was relegated to spot duty after missing four weeks of practice, leaving Sidney Thornton as the Steelers' starting halfback.

The defense went into the game missing Joe Greene at left defensive tackle. He was replaced by Gary Dunn, so the only original members of the Steel Curtain to start the 1979 season were Mel Blount, L.C. Greenwood, Jack Ham, Jack Lambert and Mike Wagner.

Greenwood injured his knee during the opener and was replaced by Tom Beasley. Nickel cornerback J.T. Thomas was also injured and replaced by rookie Dwayne Woodruff. Quarterback Terry Bradshaw sprained his big toe and missed a few series in the first half. He was replaced by Mike Kruczek. Left guard Sam Davis pulled a hamstring but remained in the game.

The Steelers were sloppy, but won in overtime, 16-13. Thornton scored both touchdowns, Dunn had three sacks and Woodruff intercepted a pass. Rookie kicker Matt Bahr missed

Terry Bradshaw shook off injuries in three of the first four games to lead the Steelers to a 4-0 start.

an extra-point attempt early in the game but came through with a 41-yard field goal in overtime.

New Sack Dance

Even in college at Miami, Florida, Gary Dunn never had three quarterback sacks in one game. That's why he looked quizzically at teammate John Banaszak when he suggested Dunn have a sack dance ready for the Monday night game in New England.

After Joe Greene twisted his knee in pregame warmups, assistant head coach George Perles told Dunn he was starting that night. Banaszak approached Dunn next.

"You know how guys are doing that stuff these days," Banaszak said. "If you're out there and you get a sack, you have to do one."

"Let me think about it," said Dunn. "If I get a sack, I'll come up with something."

After his first sack of Patriots quarterback Steve Grogan, Dunn did nothing.

"I was just happy to get one," he said.

Dunn sacked Grogan again, and again did nothing.

"I told John, 'If I get one more sack, watch me. I'm going to do a thing here.'"

Dunn sacked Grogan a third time and followed through on his promise.

"I got the third sack and did this crank thing," Dunn said. "I swung my arm around and did like this punch deal. I'd sacked Grogan and was kind of leaning up over him and I swung my arm around to do this dance thing. Well, Grogan stood up and I punched him right in the face. And the ref threw the flag and this brawl almost broke out. I came to the

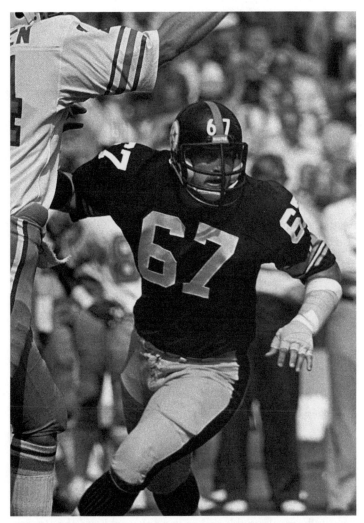

Gary Dunn had three sacks in the season opener against New England as a last-minute replacement for Joe Greene. Dunn eventually became the starter that season at right defensive tackle.

sideline and my coach was screaming at me, 'What in the world?' I said 'Hey, I was trying to do a sack dance and it didn't work out too well.' So that was the first and the last of the sack dance."

Repercussions?

"I got a lot of mail," Dunn said. "It was almost all positive, from Steeler fans. I got some from New England, too. It wasn't too positive."

Kick Start to a Career

Matt Bahr believes kicking field goals is more of a mental exercise than a physical one. But he couldn't have been too mentally sound as he lined up for a 41-yard field goal in overtime of his first professional start. Bahr had missed an extra-point attempt in the second quarter that left the Steelers trailing the New England Patriots, 7-6. He'd also missed a 44-yard field-goal attempt in the third quarter.

"My first game could easily have been my last one," he said. "A Monday night game, defending Super Bowl champs, winners three of the last five years. I could just hear Howard Cosell up in the booth writing my epitaph, 'He'll never kick again.'"

Fortunately for Bahr, the Steelers held the Patriots in overtime and then drove to the 24-yard line. On fourth and two, Chuck Noll wondered aloud whether the Steelers should go for it or let the rookie kick again.

"Aw, give him a chance," Jack Ham told Noll.

Noll sent the field-goal unit on the field and the Patriots called a timeout.

"Jack Lambert was on the protection team, the left wing," said Bahr. "During the timeout—this was the first time Jack

Lambert ever spoke to me—he said, 'Matt, we have all the confidence in the world in you.' That really meant a lot. Whether it helped, I don't know, but I've certainly never forgotten it. It showed you why he was the great player he was. That's why he was a great teammate."

Good thing Bahr didn't hear the rest of Lambert's little pep talk.

"After Jack came back to the line to block," said Randy Grossman, "he turned to me and said, 'You know, if he misses this kick I'm going to rip his head off.'

"Maybe he was afraid of scaring Matt, I don't know."

Fortunately for Bahr, he made the field goal and lived to kick another day.

BEASLEY STRIKES OIL

Joe Greene said his injured knee felt better just as he watched Gary Dunn record his third sack the previous Monday night.

L.C. Greenwood felt the same way about his knee while watching his replacement, Tom Beasley, tear up the Houston Oilers.

Beasley made 11 tackles in a 38-7 win—the Steelers' best performance of the first half of the 1979 regular season. The Steelers held 1978 MVP and Rookie of the Year running back Earl Campbell to 38 yards with a defensive performance reminiscent of the 1974 season.

Sports Illustrated broke down the statistics in terms of inches. Prior to quarterback Dan Pastorini leaving the field on a stretcher in the third quarter, the Oilers ran 35 plays for 17 yards, or an average of 17.5 inches per play. On 14 first-down plays called by Pastorini, the Oilers netted a negative three yards. Pastorini completed four of 16 passes for 16 yards. The Steelers recorded five sacks and had five interceptions.

Greene was asked after the game if he'd ever seen the Steelers play better defense.

"Hell, yes," he said. "This is the Steelers you're talking about."

Because of his work at the line of scrimmage, Beasley received one of three game balls awarded.

"He's a smart kid from Virginia Tech and he quickly understood they were going to run the ball at him," said John Banaszak. "They were going to run the ball at Tom Beasley and he stood up and held his ground and had a great ball game."

George Perles felt Beasley played well enough to earn NFL Player of the Week honors, and was livid when it was given to Steve Grogan.

"That's crap," Perles told the *McKeesport Daily News*. "It should've been Beasley. Hell, he was inside Campbell's jersey all afternoon."

WAGNER SURVIVES THREAT

In the AFC Championship Game the previous season, Steelers free safety Mike Wagner measured up the pass and realized Oilers tight end Mike Barber would not catch it. So Wagner dove to the turf to avoid contact, but instead hit Barber's ankle. As Barber was helped from the field, he pointed at Wagner and then shouted at him from the sideline throughout the remainder of the game. Prior to the 1979 early-season meeting, Barber promised revenge.

"I don't intend to let it slide," he wrote in the *Houston Chronicle*. "I intend to get him back."

In the pregame conference call, Oilers Coach Bum Phillips said: "Barber's not going to be looking for Wagner, but you know damn well that if he gets a chance to put him in the nickel bleachers, he'll do it."

Before the game, Wagner told Barber he was sorry about the injury. There was no incident during the game, but Wagner intercepted two passes and was awarded a game ball.

Wagner was probably more worried about Earl Campbell than Barber anyway. In Campbell's first game against the Steelers in 1978, the 232-pound running back gained 89 yards, scored three touchdowns and administered a beating to Wagner.

"Mike made 20 tackles that night," said Banaszak. "He was pretty beat up. He came back to the huddle begging us to help him out. We told him it was beneath him to beg."

BANNY'S CAREER PLAY

The Steelers gave out three game balls to defensive players after demolishing the Oilers. John Banaszak earned the third for his interception in the third quarter.

"That was a career highlight for me," said the defensive end. "It was a thing of beauty."

With the Steelers leading 17-0, the Oilers were pinned at their 15-yard line and faced second down and 20. Pastorini dropped back to find tight end Mike Barber on a slant, but Jack Ham knocked Barber out of the pattern and Pastorini scrambled to his left. Meanwhile, defensive tackle Steve Furness ran a stunt and Banaszak was stalemated at the line of scrimmage.

"That's the way I remember it anyway," Banaszak said. "Others may have said I was stuffed at the line of scrimmage."

Outside linebacker Loren Toews rushed off the corner and tipped Pastorini's flare pass in the air.

"I'd like to tell you that it was tremendous athleticism on my part, a tremendous one-handed interception, but the ball fell into my breadbasket," Banaszak said. "All of the sudden the ball was in my hands at the 10, and I said, 'Well, I'm going to score.' I had those illusions of grandeur. I started running with

John Banaszak (76) is congratulated by Tom Beasley (65) after intercepting a Dan Pastorini pass and returning it to the 5-yard line. It was the only interception of Banaszak's career.

it and between myself and the goal line was Pastorini. Well, Dante made a big mistake. Never tackle a big man in his mid-section. Either hit him high and try to collar him down or you hit him low. He tried to hit me belt-high and not only did I hit him, but Earl Campbell, who would've caught me anyway, hit me from behind and both of us landed on top of Pastorini on the five-yard line. I was five yards away from glory, absolute glory.

"The ironic thing about it was poor Pastorini, with the weight of myself and Earl Campbell bowling over the top of him, lay prone on the field and they had to come and take him off on a stretcher. That was another game where Pastorini got hauled off the field. God, he should've let me score."

It turned out to be the only interception of Banaszak's seven-year pro career.

"At least I can say I returned it all the way to the five."

ROCKY PONDERS HIS ROLE

Rocky Bleier is a good guy, a war hero for crying out loud, but that doesn't mean he liked what was going on early in the 1979 season.

In two and a half games, Bleier had carried the ball three times. He'd been replaced by Sidney Thornton and didn't like it, still doesn't 25 years later.

"It bugged me," Bleier said. "And it still bugs me how coaching staffs don't disseminate information. There's obviously a plan they have, something they would like to do and to achieve."

It was obvious the Steelers planned to phase Thornton into the 1979 lineup. A minor knee injury to Bleier in training camp helped further the plan along.

"It was just a matter of grooming younger players," said Bleier, who couldn't accept that as an answer. Not after what he'd gone through to get there.

Bleier, of course, was the only NFL player to see active duty in Vietnam. After making the Steelers out of Notre Dame in 1968, Bleier was drafted into service and was on patrol near Chu Lai when he was shot in the left thigh by the Viet Cong. As he crawled toward the rest of his platoon, a grenade sent shrapnel into his right leg and foot.

"When he got back," Steelers trainer Ralph Berlin said in *Pittsburgh Steelers: The Official Team History*, "he looked like something that had come out of a concentration camp. But the kid wanted to play."

After several operations, Bleier regenerated the nerve and regained his strength and flexibility to the point that in 1970 the Steelers kept him on injured reserve.

A week before training camp in 1971, Bleier pulled a hamstring and was out four weeks. The team's chief surgeon recommended he retire, but Bleier begged him not to tell Chuck Noll. He made the team as a member of the taxi squad and played sparingly on special teams.

In the preseason of 1972, Bleier led the team in rushing and carried the ball once during the regular season.

In 1973, Bleier was in the best shape of his life, thanks to yoga and Russian speed training, and he carried the ball three times. He wanted to retire after the season but was talked out of it by Andy Russell.

"Don't make it so easy for them," Russell told him.

Bleier led the team in preseason rushing again in 1974 and, after inseason injuries to Franco Harris, Frenchy Fuqua and Steve Davis, made his first start. The next week, Harris returned, but Bleier remained in the lineup because of his blocking. He moved over to halfback and was one of the key players in the Steelers' first Super Bowl.

Bleier held onto the job until 1979, when the Steelers developed other plans. But as he'd done throughout the early part of the decade, Bleier didn't make it easy for the coaching staff and eventually regained his job.

"Sidney was so strong and Greg (Hawthorne) was the slasher-style runner that we haven't seen since Preston Pearson, even to this day," Bleier said. "But they never sat me down to say, 'This is how it's evolving. This is the role we want you to play.' They don't tell you that. So anyway, the season starts and I don't start. It's a blow to your ego. In retrospect, I got some vindication. I played well in the second half of the season and then started in the Super Bowl, so it was a vindication of sorts."

The comeback began in the third game. During the second half against the St. Louis Cardinals, Bleier replaced an injured Harris and gained 73 yards on 13 carries. He also caught two passes for 44 yards and scored a touchdown to lead the Steelers back from a 21-7 deficit. Matt Bahr kicked a 20-yard field goal with 13 seconds left for a 24-21 Steelers win.

"I single-handedly won that game," Bleier said with a laugh. "The other thing that happened, which wouldn't have if I'd have been starting early in the season, was my 70-yard run against the Cleveland Browns. I wouldn't have been the fullback in a third-down situation and that turned out to be my greatest run, so I have a soft spot in my heart for the Cleveland Browns. If it wasn't for them, my longest run would've been 28 yards."

Oh, Hell

Jon Kolb was in his 11th season with the Steelers in 1979 and a chronic pinched nerve in his neck was causing him terrible pain. A year earlier, Kolb had played through the pain, which only subsided after a week off.

In 1979, Kolb was hoping to sit out the entire fourth game of the season, against the Baltimore Colts, but was needed in the fourth quarter because the Colts were teeing off on Terry Bradshaw. And since Kolb was using more brains than brawn

Bennie Cunningham (89), shown here versus the Bengals, was the hero of the 17-13 win over the Colts. His acting job on a throwback screen resulted in the game-winning touchdown.

that series anyway, Chuck Noll called a play he felt could work against the aggressive Colts defensive linemen.

Back in the days when Ray Mansfield was selling the play to defenders, it was called the 'Oh, Hell' screen pass. By the late seventies, tight end Bennie Cunningham had become the con man for 5-38 Middle Throwback Screen.

The Steelers trailed 13-10 with less than six minutes remaining when Cunningham blocked down and then purposely fell down. Kolb, meanwhile, slipped out to block Colts linebacker Stan White. Bradshaw hit Cunningham with the short pass and Kolb sprung him for a 28-yard touchdown. Kolb then resumed his seat on the bench in painful silence as the Steelers held on for the win.

Franco Harris missed the game with an ankle injury and Sidney Thornton rushed for 129 yards on 13 carries. He also had a 75-yard run but did not score. Thornton was caught at the Colts 10 and the Steelers fumbled on the next play.

"I just ran out of gas," he said.

The game was the best of Thornton's six-year NFL career.

For the Steelers, it was a franchise-record 12th consecutive win, but another lethargic one. Joe Greene was asked how long he believed the patched-up Steelers could continue to win close games.

"Until hell freezes over," he said.

PASS THE POTASSIUM, PLEASE

After St. Louis Cardinals wide receiver J.V. Cain collapsed and died on a practice field in the summer of 1979, the pathologist who performed the autopsy theorized the death was due to too much potassium in Cain's bloodstream. Even though Cain's death was officially attributed to a hereditary heart condition, the Steelers responded by substituting tap water in lieu of potassium-rich Gatorade.

But after Lynn Swann and Gerry Mullins left the Colts game with hamstring pulls, becoming the sixth and seventh players to suffer the injury in 1979, Chuck Noll announced the team was going back to Gatorade.

Noll said the Steelers had acted on "misinformation." Noll explained to reporters that the absence of salt and potassium in the players' fluids caused an electrolytic imbalance.

"Do you know what I'm talking about?" Noll asked.

"No," said one reporter.

"Neither do I," Noll said, "Let's let it go at that."

The Steelers resumed drinking Gatorade the next day at practice. Jim Smith, working in place of Swann, left that practice with a pulled hamstring.

Hell Freezes Over

Mike Wagner made the calls in the Steelers secondary throughout the 1970s. He also made the call 25 years later that best summed up the '79 season.

"Our physical abilities may have started to decline," he said, "but the will to win and the heart of some of these players was amazing to me."

Through the first quarter of the season, the Steelers played one good game, and yet were 4–0.

They did it with an offensive line that hadn't been intact since the second day of training camp. They did it with Joe Greene, L.C. Greenwood and Dwight White missing time with injuries. They did it as Jack Lambert played with a separated shoulder. They did it with Franco Harris missing time, with Lynn Swann missing time, with Terry Bradshaw leaving and then returning in three of the four games. They did it with the will to win and heart.

But then hell froze over. The Steelers lost to the Philadelphia Eagles, 17-14, in a game billed as the biggest between the teams since the 1947 divisional title game. At least the 4-1 Eagles looked at it that way. The Steelers fell to 4-1 and looked ahead to playing their rivals, the Cleveland Browns, the following week. But even after beating the Browns, the Steelers remained flat. What followed the Oct. 7 win in Cleveland was the most shocking loss of the Chuck Noll era.

TURNPIKE RIVALRY

If you're taking the trip up the turnpike to Memorial Stadium to watch the Steelers play the Cleveland Browns, count on three things: rain, fights and vandalism.

And if you're in the media, count on working in a cramped trailer of a locker room with fans banging on the metallic walls and your tape recorder not picking up any of the interviews.

And if you're a player, count on this:

"That infield dirt and the stuff would get underneath your jersey and you'd get little, tiny cuts all over," said Gary Dunn. "Then we'd go in the locker room and they'd have, for the whole team, four showers and only two of them worked and the water was barely warm."

Hated it, right?

"Oh, no," Dunn said. "I liked playing in Cleveland. The Cleveland-Pittsburgh thing was good, real good."

"You'd start down that rickety, musty, old walkway to the field," was how Jack Lambert described Memorial Stadium to the *Akron Beacon Journal*, "and you could smell the mustard and the hot dogs, you could feel and hear the cold wind whipping in from the lake, and there, right before you, was a real football field, a grass field. It was great."

In mid October of 1979, the Steelers played the Browns for first place in the AFC Central. They were both 4-1, as were the Houston Oilers. It was a big game for the Browns, who were hoping to regain their place as kings of the division.

In 1967, the NFL went to four divisions and the Browns controlled the Century Division, topping the Steelers, New York Giants and St. Louis Cardinals all three years.

The NFL merged with the AFL in 1970 and the Cincinnati Bengals won the first AFC Central Division title. They were succeeded by the Browns in 1971. The Steelers finished first in 1972 and then won five in a row from 1974 through 1978. While the Steelers won three NFL championships during that streak, the Browns finished last in the division three times.

Yet the Browns took the Steelers into overtime at Three Rivers Stadium in 1978 and finished 9-7. This, the Browns felt, could be their year, and Memorial Stadium was certainly the place to beat an old, fat-cat bunch of Steelers. After all, it's the place where Turkey Jones almost broke Terry Bradshaw's neck in 1976. It's the place where Mike Wagner did break his neck in 1977. Joe Greene was ejected from a 1975 game in Cleveland. Lambert was ejected from the 1978 game.

The Browns had beaten the Dallas Cowboys only two weeks before, and the headline in the Cleveland paper the day before this game announced "Steelers are hurting badly; ready for knockout punch."

Well, the old fat cats scored the game's first 27 points and rolled to a 51-35 win in front of 81,260 brawling drunks. The win, coupled with the Cardinals' upset win over the Oilers, left the Steelers alone in first place. The knockout punch would have to wait another year.

IT ALL STARTS UP FRONT

Dan Radakovich coached the Steelers offensive line from 1974-77 before leaving with Bud Carson to join the staff of the Los Angeles Rams. No one outside the offices of Three Rivers Stadium knew the Steelers' front wall like "Bad Rad." Here, 25 years later, is his scouting report:

"(Mike) Webster was great. I had Webster his first four years. He alternated with (Ray) Mansfield the first two years.

"They had Jon Kolb, of course. He was a great tackle, a left tackle. If he'd ever been a guard, they'd still be talking about the greatest guard in history. He was the fastest offensive lineman in the NFL. He ran a 4.7 on grass but we needed a left tackle and left tackle's the most important position in football. See, he wasn't as big as the normal left tackle. He was 6-2, 263, but he was also the strongest lineman in football.

"And Sam Davis was playing. He was a great athlete. Not big, but coordinated, could run faster backwards than I could forward.

"You had Gerry Mullins who played first-string guard and tackle. When I became offensive line coach I put him on first team.

"You had Larry Brown at right tackle. Larry Brown, you talk to Steelers players today from that era or even later, like Emil Boures, they've never seen anybody better than Larry Brown. In their opinion, Larry Brown wasn't just a great tackle, he was the best who ever lived. He was a tight end and I made him a tackle. He started in '76. He was a great tackle. Ask anybody.

"They had a helluva line. They had the only two linemen who started all four Super Bowls and won them, Kolb and Mullins. I told that to the Southern Cal coaches. 'You have the only guard in history that ever started and won four Super Bowls. You're supposed to be Offensive Line U and you don't even have his picture up there.' They had no idea who it was. I said, Gerry Mullins. He was a tight end there. They still don't have his picture up."

For the first time in 1979, this group played together in Cleveland. The result was a bludgeoning. The Steelers rolled up 361 yards rushing, a team record to this day. Offensive line coach Rollie Dotsch was awarded the game ball for the job his men did in controlling the trenches.

The Steelers nearly became the first team in NFL history with three 100-yard rushers in one game. Franco Harris broke out of his slump with 153 yards, followed by Sidney Thornton with 98 and Rocky Bleier with 81 on only four carries, thanks to his 70-yard touchdown run in the fourth quarter. It put the Steelers ahead by 44-21 and naturally put the spotlight squarely on the backs—where it didn't belong.

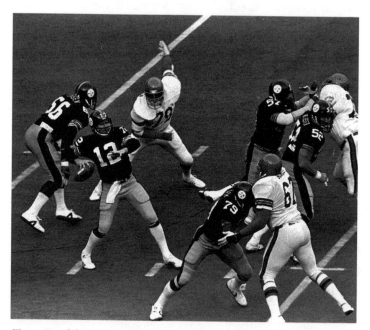

Terry Bradshaw receives protection from Larry Brown (79), Mike Webster (52), Sam Davis (57), and Ted Petersen (66).

"Being overlooked is just part of being an offensive line-man," Mullins said after the game.

Napalm in the Morning

Vandals normally wait until game day at Memorial Stadium to slice and dice tires of cars bearing Pennsylvania license plates. In 1979, they struck the night before.

Police in Cleveland investigated more than 30 autos damaged on the premises of the hotel at which the Steelers and several of their fans stayed the night before the game. An estimated 200 tires had been slashed, including those on some of the fan buses.

The Steelers' buses escaped without incident, and most of the passengers went home in a good mood. Most, that is, except for Jim Smith. The third-year receiver had overcome his hamstring injury to catch two passes in the game, but he couldn't overcome the second-hand smoke threatening to overtake the bus.

"Put out that cigarette," Smith bellowed after reporter Vic Ketchman lit one up.

It was at the tail-end of those carefree days for smokers, but Smith was a charter member of the smoking police.

Ketchman turned around to put a face with the voice and saw Smith. Sitting next to Smith was John Stallworth, who frequently bummed cigarettes from the writers.

Ketchman nodded at Smith and with his eyes said to Stallworth, "Thanks for the help, pal."

Stallworth offered the helpless look that said: "I know. I feel bad."

A couple of minutes after Ketchman had snuffed out his cigarette, a big puff of smoke billowed up over his head from behind.

"Oh, boy," Ketchman thought. "Smith is going to jump his ass."

But nothing was said.

"I've got to find out who's behind me," Ketchman thought as he turned slowly. Behind him was Jack Lambert with a cigarette in his mouth and a big smile on his face. Lambert took a deep drag, inhaled and blew out another cloud of smoke.

Ketchman laughed. "Jimmy Smith never said a word as Jack smoked all the way to Pittsburgh."

Out-Bungling the Bungles

According to Chuck Noll, from 1972 to 1979 the Steelers played 60 games against teams with losing records and won 59 times. The one loss came against the Cincinnati Bengals in Week 7 of the '79 season.

The Steelers were at their healthiest point of the season, were wary of the 0-6 Bengals after winning by only 7-6 the previous season, and promised there wouldn't be a letdown.

There was.

The Steelers fumbled nine times and lost it seven times in a 34-10 loss at Riverfront Stadium.

The Bengals scored 20 points in a span of 1:54 in the second quarter thanks to three Steelers fumbles. At halftime, the Bengals led by 27-3 and Noll was at a loss.

"I'll always remember Chuck in that locker room," said Jack Ham. "He said, 'If I wouldn't know any better, I would've thought you guys were throwing this game.'"

"I looked at Mike Wagner like, 'Did he just accuse us of putting money on the game?'"

"I remember that," said Wagner. "Chuck was a very laid-back motivator, very serious, consistent, not a rah-rah guy. He used to frequently come in at halftime and tell us, 'You can't just turn the switch on. You can't just all of the sudden play great football. You've got to play great football for four quarters. You've got to practice hard, study hard.' So it surprised us coach would accuse us of that but it was probably just Chuck digging deep to get our attention.

"We had a lot of pretty smart people on our football team and I think it was easy for Chuck to communicate in that way to us, by taking that kind of approach. You know he's not being serious, but just by making that kind of statement, I mean, Chuck rarely did anything that wasn't premeditated. I always felt he wrote everything down he was going to say that day in a spiral binder. He used to show up in meetings with his little spiral binder notebook and quite honestly, I always felt he'd go back through six or seven years of notes to pick out his speech because I'd say, 'This one sounds familiar.' That's why I say the players were kind of smart, so I think in a way we were a little surprised when Chuck threw that one at us. But I think we were also kind of humored by it.

"In a way it was a compliment. It was a way of Chuck saying, 'You guys are playing terribly. You're much better than this.' He was accusing us of not playing up to our potential.

"You know," Wagner continued, "being on a football field and being on a sideline are two different things. I'm sure it's always hard to be a coach because they think they know what's going on but they really don't know. They don't know how hard you got hit in the head that last play. So I guess I was always the kind of player who took stuff tongue in cheek, much to Chuck's chagrin. Jack and I have always been good buddies, so that's probably why we had our little eye contact and shook our heads."

The Steelers bounded out of the locker room and promptly fumbled three snaps in their first two second-half possessions, losing two of them. After the game, Noll told reporters, "Too bad it wasn't raining. We'd have had some excuses."

CHAPTER VI

FINAL ENCORE:
THE CURTAIN RISES AGAIN

"Ron Johnson, he's a product of the television age, came into the huddle and said, 'C'mon, Steel Curtain, let's get it going!' He hasn't lived that down yet."

—Chuck Noll

THE HUDDLE

L.C. Greenwood is one laid-back cat. Feel free to ask him just about anything these days.

L.C., how's your business doing?

"Well, the doors are open. Things could really be a lot better, but I'm blessed that I can keep the doors open."

Which was the best Steelers team?

"The '76 Steelers. I think that was the greatest team of all time. I know it's kind of debatable because we didn't win the Super Bowl or didn't get to the Super Bowl, but as far as the team and accomplishments as a Pittsburgh Steelers team, I think that was the greatest team we had."

Who was your most interesting teammate?

"I can't really single one out. That's what made our team great. We had all these distinctive characters. Ernie was different; Dwight, man. It was so interesting being in the huddle. I think a lot of guys miss that, being in the huddle on Sundays when things were happening like they happened. You'd be standing in the huddle and there's Joe being the president of the company. And then you've got Dwight arguing because something was happening with the person he's playing against. And then you've got Ernie all focused on trying to hit somebody. Then you go in the secondary and you had Mel over there by himself, didn't care what everybody else was doing. The linebackers, Ham didn't know the plays half the time and I had to remember the plays so I could tell him at the line of scrimmage, so I had to pay attention to help him out. Then Lambert's back there fighting with the coaches to get the plays in.

"It was all kinds of things. It was just a great bunch of guys and we went out there on the field and had a bunch of fun playing together as a group. All these different personalities, plus we were able to get to the bottom line and the bottom line was to try to win the football game. We were able to put aside all that stuff when the ball was snapped and do what we had to do and everybody wanted to get after the football."

BACK TO BASICS

The defense had looked like anything but the Steel Curtain heading into a Monday night game against the Denver Broncos. In back-to-back games against the Cleveland Browns and Cincinnati Bengals, the Steelers allowed 69 points, the most in consecutive games since midway through the 1-13 1969 season, Chuck Noll's first in Pittsburgh.

In promising a "back-to-basics" approach for the Broncos game, Noll said: "We may have to go back to training camp."

He wanted better defensive play, in particular a better pass rush, better pass defense from right outside linebacker Dirt Winston and better overall play from strong safety Donnie Shell. Noll hinted he may replace Shell with J.T. Thomas. The only player praised for his tackling was kicker Matt Bahr, who had three unassisted special teams tackles in less than half a season.

Matt Bahr?

"One time there was a breakthrough," Bahr said, "and the return man had two blockers in front of him. All three of them knew I was a kicker and they were smiling. The blockers were fighting each other to wipe me out and I was backpedaling, but in their enthusiasm to knock me over they knocked each other over and the running back stumbled over them and I was able to get him out of bounds."

Even though the Steelers had an extra day to rest before the Monday nighter, boot camp began immediately. On Monday, the Steelers ran through a 37-play practice with enough intensity to force a scuffle between Dwight White and Jon Kolb. Practice ended with a series of 350-yard sprints.

"It was the epitome of fundamentals," said assistant head coach George Perles.

Former quarterback Terry Hanratty had been through those "back-to-basics" weeks in his time. He was working for E.F. Hutton in suburban Denver at the time, and when Hanratty talked to the *Pittsburgh Press*, people listened.

"I'll bet there was a real quiet atmosphere at practice this week," Hanratty said. "Like the calm before a tornado hits."

FUNNEL CLOUDS AT THE CONFLUENCE

Strange words came from unexpected places after the 6-2 Steelers ripped through the Denver Broncos, 42-7.

Red Miller, coach of the 5-3 Broncos and less than two years removed from a Super Bowl appearance, called it "my worst, my most humiliating defeat in 30 years of coaching. I don't see how anybody can stomach this and live with it."

Perhaps more surprisingly, the normally even-keeled Chuck Noll was elated after the game. "That's the Steeler team I know," Noll said proudly. He was awarded the game ball by Terry Bradshaw "for getting us ready."

The most surprising words, at least to the ears of sensitive Steelers fans, came from game announcer Howard Cosell.

The previous week, after the Pirates had won the World Series, Cosell dubbed Pittsburgh the "City of Champions." Cosell couldn't say it enough during the Monday night game. He even mocked Pittsburgh reporters who'd written stories suggesting Franco Harris had lost a step. Harris gained 121 yards on 17 carries.

Cosell also made a prediction on the upcoming game against the Dallas Cowboys.

"Dallas will win the game," he said. "But I don't think that's relevant, because the Steelers will beat them in the Super Bowl. I think Pittsburgh's gonna win because it has the greatest people in football. But it's impossible for human beings to be as up, as the Steelers were tonight, every week."

TALKING TRASH

Thomas "Hollywood" Henderson may have invented this blight on the modern game—trash talking—at the previous Super Bowl, but it was the Steelers coaching staff who took the ball and ran with it. Chuck Noll mocked Tom Landry's whining over a bad call, and Noll's top assistant, George Perles, was responsible for filling up the Dallas Cowboys' bulletin board for the October 28, 1979 meeting at Three Rivers Stadium.

"I really think their whole philosophy is wrong," Perles had said after the Steelers beat the Cowboys in Super Bowl XIII. "I really think they get more satisfaction out of fooling someone than knocking their block off. I personally think they're the biggest bunch of hypocrites that ever hit the pike."

Perles went on to predict the Cowboys would win the preseason game in '79, "but we'll kick the heck out of them in the regular season."

The quotes, of course, were played back before the regular-season meeting.

"Do you have to keep reminding everybody about that?" Perles asked Stellino of the *Post-Gazette*.

But Perles went two for two as a prognosticator. The Steelers did lose the preseason game and then stuffed the Cowboys, 14-3, in Week 9 of the '79 season.

Perles also proved to be more than a seer. His defense was outrageous. It held the Cowboys to 79 yards rushing, knocked quarterback Roger Staubach out of the game with a concussion and halfback Preston Pearson out with rib and knee injuries. The great Tony Dorsett had his string of four 100-yard

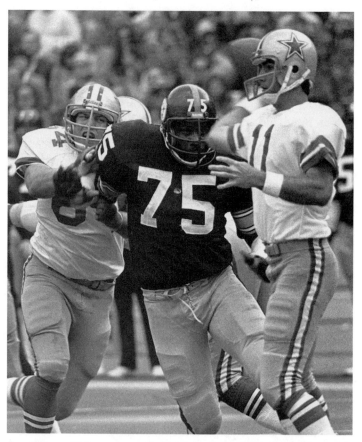

Joe Greene (75) pressures Dallas quarterback Danny White, who admitted after the game the Cowboys "were intimidated."

games stopped. He gained 17 yards on 11 first-half carries and finished with 73 yards on 19 carries.

"We were intimidated," said back-up Cowboys quarterback Danny White, who spoke as if he were a Perles disciple.

"The way it looked today, it's going to be tough for us to beat them without changing our whole program," White said. "It's just a difference in philosophies, the physical game against the intelligence game. They don't draft players who can handle a complicated game plan. They draft guys who they can put in the line and say, 'Hit that guy. Knock him down.' They draft guys named Dirt."

Sports Illustrated ran with the theme. In a cover story titled "Super Bowl XIII?", the author listed the Cowboys' trick plays from the Super Bowl before enumerating those from the October 28 game. The Cowboys tried to win at Three Rivers Stadium with a halfback option pass, a Statue of Liberty and a fake punt, all of which netted minus 10 yards thanks to a holding penalty.

"We got a look at the whole computer," said John Banaszak.

Sports Illustrated wondered if the message would get through to the Cowboys.

"Hey Tom," the author concluded, "the Steelers know which shell the pea is under."

A GUY NAMED DIRT

When Dennis "Dirt" Winston replaced the injured combo of Robin Cole and Loren Toews at right outside linebacker against the Cleveland Browns, quarterback Brian Sipe attacked him through the air. In all, Sipe ended up with five touchdown passes and more passing yards, 365, than the Steelers had allowed in four years.

Winston normally played middle linebacker and played it well. While filling in for Jack Lambert, he'd caused back-to-back turnovers—even scored on an interception return—against Houston. Winston had also been awarded game balls in the two previous games against the Dallas Cowboys.

Winston made it three in a row with his 10 solo tackles against the Cowboys in 1979. Chuck Noll called him the best player on the field that day, and naturally the national reporters wanted to know the origin of his nickname.

"Oh, that was something I got in college," was all Winston would say.

Steelers historians know Winston earned his nickname at Arkansas because of his, well, dirty play. "I've taken a whole lot of cheap shots at different people," he said as a rookie fifth-round draft pick in 1977.

However, as the Cowboys ran repeatedly at Winston, the supposed weak link, CBS announcers Pat Summerall and Tom Brookshier explained the nickname came about because Winston "likes to play in the dirt." Winston was fine with it, since he hoped to clean up his reputation. And it was a reputation that was growing with his teammates.

"Dennis Winston was really a great player to have on the team," said Mike Wagner. "He was a lot of fun. He was fierce as could be and he wanted to win at all cost, but he was always fun because Lambert always used to tease Dirt, and they had a real nice rivalry that fed up into the team."

Teasing?

"Just the way they would be fierce with each other and pick on each other," Wagner said. "You know, there's a tremendous amount of stress when you're expected to win championships and you're trying to repeat. It's just hard to explain it.

"When people see us old athletes socializing or competing on the golf course, they think from afar that we don't like each other, that we're angry. I call it locker-room humor. If you don't pick on somebody, you're going to get picked on. So you've got to have thick skin to be an athlete in team sports. That's just your deal with your teammates. Then you've got to have thick skin to deal with your coaches. Then you've got to have thick skin to deal with the fans. But Lambert had a way of getting players comfortable by drawing attention to them, by pointing out maybe something they did silly or did wrong. He'd embarrass them a little bit but then he'd do something to encourage them and make them want to go prove themselves."

FUZZY MEMORIES

John Elway made a forgettable NFL debut against the Steelers in 1983. He completed one of eight passes for 14 yards and left the field battered, replaced by Steve DeBerg.

Elway's most vivid memory of the game is that of middle linebacker Jack Lambert.

"He had no teeth and he was slobbering all over," Elway told reporters prior to the 1997 AFC Championship Game in Pittsburgh. "I'm thinking, 'You can have your money back, just get me out of here, let me go be an accountant.' I can't even tell you how badly I wanted out of there."

Cris Collinsworth also remembers the first time he went up against Lambert. As a rookie with the Cincinnati Bengals in 1981, Collinsworth ran a pattern across the middle and was nearly knocked cold by Lambert, who warned him: "Collinsworth, don't you ever come across here again."

Collinsworth went back to his huddle with a big smile on his face. His teammates couldn't understand why.

"Jack Lambert knows my name," he explained.

In 1979, Lambert was in the midst of one of his best seasons, albeit one of his most painful. In Week 10, he led the Steelers with 11 total tackles in a 38-7 dismantling of the 6-4 Washington Redskins. It was yet another outstanding defensive performance by the Steelers, who'd allowed 17 points in a three-game span.

Lambert would finish the season with team highs in interceptions (six), solo tackles (119), assists (46) and of course total tackles (165). He made 64 more tackles than runner-up Jack Ham, and did most of it with a separated shoulder. The injury occurred before the third game of the season when he collided in practice with Thornton, the Thundering Bull.

Lambert didn't miss a game that season, but didn't want to talk about it, or anything else for that matter. Lambert's post-football interviews are few and far between.

Lambert retired after dislocating his big toe in 1984. He was inducted into the Pro Football Hall of Fame in 1990. He lives on an 85-acre farm north of Pittsburgh near Kittanning.

Lambert met his wife, Lisa, a volleyball player from Clemson University and Pittsburgh's Plum High School, at a nearby bar. She was in the company of an older gentleman, which didn't discourage Lambert from sending a couple of drinks their way. According to the *Akron Beacon Journal*, Lambert was sent a message in return.

"The lady thanks you," said the bartender, "and so does her father."

"I just quietly pumped my fist and said, 'Yes,'" said Lambert.

Jack Lambert (58) intercepted six passes in 1979. It's still a team record for linebackers.

Thinning Up Top

One of the Rooney boys not affiliated with the team likes to offer up a prayer of hope to those around him whenever the Steelers fall behind these days.

"You always have a chance," he says. "The other team has coaches, too."

Imagine the panic of one of these modern-day control freaks if he were to be transported back in time and put in charge of the 1979 Steelers secondary.

Free safety Mike Wagner had just been placed on injured reserve with a hip injury and cornerback Ron Johnson was out for the Washington game with a concussion. That left

Donnie Shell at strong safety—and the Steelers had been thinking of benching him only two weeks ago—and Mel Blount at right cornerback. J.T. Thomas was moved from cornerback to free safety for the first time in his six-year career. Rookie Dwayne Woodruff would start at left cornerback. That left Larry Anderson, a second-year pro kept only because of his kick-return skills, to play in the sub, nickel and dime packages.

Sub, nickel and dime packages?

Not in 1979, when the Steelers only used a fifth defensive back on third and very long.

So the Steelers went into the 10th game of the season a bit thin in the secondary. Not that it mattered. Quarterback Joe Theisman came out throwing to 240-pound tailback John Riggins, who led the Redskins with four catches.

Jack Pardee's defensive game plan was equally puzzling. He played a nine-man front to stop Franco Harris, so Terry Bradshaw completed 11 passes to wide receivers John Stallworth and Lynn Swann for 232 yards and two touchdowns, and five passes to tight ends Randy Grossman and Bennie Cunningham for 78 yards and two touchdowns. Bradshaw threw for a career regular-season high 311 yards, and the Steelers rolled up 545 yards of offense in a 38-7 win against what had been the NFL's stingiest defense.

Over the last three games, the Steelers had been the stingiest. They hadn't allowed over 100 yards team rushing in any of them and allowed only 17 total points. Shell played a key role. The 1978 Pro Bowler broke out of his slump with interceptions in each of the three games. He also sacked Theisman.

"I heard Woody (Widenhofer) was thinking about making a change," Shell said of his defensive coordinator. "I guess that's what woke me up."

ANOTHER BRICK IN THE WALL

When Donnie Shell lined up to start against the Dallas
Cowboys in Super Bowl XIII, the player he would groom one
day to follow in his footsteps as the Steelers strong safety had
just turned six years old.

"Right now I think I am a technique guy," said Lee
Flowers prior to the 2001 season. "A lot of that came from
Coach Shell."

Shell spent 14 years with the Steelers and retired following the 1987 season. Before he began his present job as the
director of player relations for the Carolina Panthers, he dab-
bled in high school coaching. He was the defensive backs
coach at his alma mater, Spring Valley High in South Carolina,
where he trained the future strong safety of the Steelers.

"Usually in high school, you just go to the ball and make
the tackle," Flowers said. "But Donnie was big on technique,
and when I went to college I was ahead of all the guys in my
class because of that."

Flowers knew Shell had been a great player with the
Steelers, but didn't realize just how great until Shell invited
some of the senior players over for dinner one night.

"He had all the game balls around his basement," Flowers
said. "Then he showed us his clips and the hit on Earl
Campbell was, whoa, unbelievable. That's the kind of hit most
safeties spend their whole career dreaming about."

In 1978, during a late-season game against the Houston
Oilers, a game the Steelers needed to win the AFC Central
Division title, Shell hit Campbell, the NFL's most feared big
back, hard enough to break several ribs. The Steelers went on
to win the game, the division and their third Super Bowl.

"That got us over the hump," said Shell. "But, no, I don't
think it was my best tackle. I made better ones. Sure, that was
a big hit. He was running and spinning off somebody when I

hit him. But my best tackle, I think, came in the 1983 Pro Bowl. Tony Dorsett caught a pass in the flat and there wasn't anybody out there but him and me. That's a scary thought. But I brought him down in the open field. That was my best tackle."

In the flat, all alone with Tony Dorsett, Shell relied on technique to get the job done. It's what Shell tried to impress upon the young Flowers as opposed to the glory of making the big, knockout blow.

"Coach Shell is not like me, running his mouth a lot," Flowers said. "He's a reserved guy, a calm guy. Besides, he didn't want to send the wrong message to a high school guy. You don't want kids out there trying to take big hits like that or giving big hits like that. He really tried to get our heads on straight and understand that we might not ever do something like this the rest of our life.

"His message was to work on studies at school. He was a big stay-in-school guy. He never had a flamboyant attitude. What he's doing now is probably the perfect job for him. I understand he's a very inspirational leader and you need a guy like that, because this is a hard business, man. All it takes is one bad play to ruin your whole career, and he's doing a good job down there making sure players understand that."

HE'S MEAN JOE AGAIN

In a game against the Houston Oilers in 1972, Mean Joe Greene recovered a fumble, blocked a field goal and sacked the quarterback five times. The Steelers won 9-3 and Greene's performance moved Chuck Noll to tears after the game.

Greene didn't incite such emotion against the Kansas City Chiefs, but he did play his best game in years.

"He made more things happen Sunday than any game this year," Noll said after the Steelers beat the Chiefs, 30-3. "This was his best game, by far, this season."

Greene was awarded his third career game ball because, as Noll said, "he got to the ball a lot, he batted balls, he forced the play."

The Steelers rolled up 30 points for the third time in the last four games, but the defense held an opponent to single digits for the fourth consecutive game. The Steelers hadn't done that since 1976. And it obviously helped the offense, which didn't have a single touchdown drive longer than 46 yards.

The 9-2 Steelers won their last four games by a composite score of 124-20, an average of 31-5. They didn't allow 100 yards rushing to a team since Cincinnati, and against the Chiefs sacked rookie quarterback Steve Fuller four times. They did it the modern way: by blitzing linebackers and safeties and letting the front four play the run.

"We are coming more now with other people because the game is changing so much," said Noll. "Pass protection has improved considerably."

Rise, Fall, Reprise of the Curtain

Dan Radakovich was a linebackers coach at Penn State before joining the Steelers in 1971 as the new defensive line coach. The unit was a team strength. But Radakovich looked around and saw better back-ups on the bench than what was being used at the time.

"The line probably did have the best players, as far as toughness and technique go, but it lacked speed," Radakovich said.

In the middle were Joe Greene and Chuck Hinton, a steady eighth-year veteran. The ends were Lloyd Voss and Ben McGee.

"The ends were very good players, but they ran probably a 5.5 or 5.6 in the 40," Radakovich said. "We had some young guys on the bench, Dwight White and L.C. Greenwood, and they both ran 4.6 on grass, and those were legitimate times, not people bullshitting like they do. So if I put them on first team, that would increase our pursuit per play by about 10 steps. So I immediately put them on first string before the first preseason game. Everybody told me I was crazy, that I was ruining them."

Radakovich moved Voss and McGee inside where they alternated with Hinton. All three were gone by the end of the 1972 season to make way for rookie Ernie Holmes. But in 1971, White was the rookie.

"Dwight was light; L.C. was light. Hell, one of the assistants told me L.C. wouldn't last a game," Radakovich said. "He said, 'Well, you shoulda seen what Butkus did to him.' I said, 'What did Butkus do to him?' He said, 'L.C. was running down on kickoff coverage and Butkus almost put him into the stands.' And I said, 'Well, hell, Butkus does that to everybody.' So that didn't worry me. I put L.C. on first string and he played well. That's when they got the nickname Steel Curtain, that year, because of how well the defensive line played."

Along came Holmes in 1972 to round the group out. But while "Fats" had a fine rookie season, he wasn't truly feared around the league—author Roy Blount, Jr. surmised in his classic book *About Three Bricks Shy of a Load*—until "the incident."

As the story goes, Holmes blew his salary and playoff money from 1972 on the typical accoutrements. Then his marriage dissolved, so he called the Steelers in March of '73 about more money. They told him to come in for a talk, but once in Pittsburgh, Holmes became stuck in traffic. By the time he reached Three Rivers Stadium, the offices were closed. So he headed back out of town. He was so tightly wound that he began firing his pistol at passing trucks in Ohio. The police gave chase and Holmes turned onto a side road, where his car broke down. He ran into the woods with a rifle and began shooting at a police helicopter, hitting one cop in the ankle. He was found and surrendered. The Steelers helped him out of the jam, and Holmes remained under psychiatric care for two months and was placed on five years' probation.

The Steel Curtain remained at peak efficiency through 1976, when, attempting to make up for a rash of injuries on the offensive side of the ball, it allowed only 28 points in the Steelers' final nine regular-season games. Included in perhaps the greatest stretch of defensive play in NFL history were five shutouts. But without Franco Harris or Rocky Bleier, they were beaten at Oakland in the AFC Championship Game.

With Greene feeling the effects of his neck injury and Holmes becoming a growing distraction, the Curtain foundered in 1977. It bounced back in 1978 with Steve Furness at right defensive tackle and John Banaszak alternating with White at right defensive end.

The 1978 version of the Steel Curtain finished third in the NFL in total defense, second against the run, but its pass defense, altered by the outlawing of contact after five yards, was 12th. It didn't prevent the Steelers from winning a third Super Bowl.

"A funny thing happened this year that illustrates things about this season," Noll said the day after Super Bowl XIII. "I can't remember what game it was, but we weren't getting after the passer. Ron Johnson, he's a product of the television age, came into the huddle and said, 'C'mon, Steel Curtain, let's get going!' He hasn't lived that down, yet."

In weeks eight through 11 of the 1979 season, the Steel Curtain had indeed gotten it going. Banaszak was playing well against both the run and pass; Furness, or "Buckethead" as he was called, was being pushed hard by Gary Dunn; Greene was outstanding in Kansas City; Greenwood had knocked Roger Staubach out of the Dallas game, his best of the season. The Curtain had indeed risen. But the San Diego Chargers loomed.

BOMBS AWAY

To look at the linescore of the San Diego Chargers' 35-7 win over the Steelers, the knee-jerk reaction is to blame the Steelers' injury-depleted secondary. Yep, what Steve Fuller couldn't do, Dan Fouts surely could. And wasn't it about time those new rules caught up with physical cover men such as Mel Blount, Ron Johnson, J.T. Thomas and Donnie Shell?

Don Coryell's Chargers were certainly the team to exploit a secondary that relied more on toughness than finesse, but Fouts, John Jefferson and Charlie Joiner only managed to put up 120 passing yards against the Steelers. The Chargers' total output was 218 yards.

No, the Chargers won because the Steelers committed eight turnovers.

Terry Bradshaw threw five interceptions against a defense that dropped its linebackers deep in order to double the Steelers' receivers.

That's right, Coryell's Chargers whipped the Steelers in '79 with defense.

The result left both teams at 9-3. Certainly, the Chargers—who finished the '78 season in a 7-1 rush after changing coaches—would be a threat in the playoffs. But would the Steelers be there? They were now tied with the Oilers for first place in the AFC Central Division, one game ahead of the Browns, who were up next at Three Rivers Stadium.

In the span of four quarters, the Steelers went from being "the greatest football team in the history of the game," as Coryell had called them, to "just another team struggling for the playoffs," as Bradshaw said afterward.

A MAD DOG HOWLS

As the Steel Curtain enjoyed a reprise of sorts, one player was left to wonder whether he fit in anymore.

"That's a situation that to this day I have heartburn about," said Dwight White, who's currently the senior managing director of the Pittsburgh branch of Mesirow Financial.

White, of course, was the legendary "Mad Dog" of the Steelers' front four. He was the blindside pass rusher. But along came John Banaszak, a quality end in his own right, and the coaching staff eased him into the lineup in 1978. By 1979, it had become a full-blown demotion for White, who alternated series with Banaszak.

"I have this theory that it had nothing to do with performance on the field, that there were some other dynamics in play," said White. "When Dan Radakovich put that line together, and it was inherited by George Perles, I think a relationship developed there that should've never gotten into the on-field performance. And I think part of the fact that people inherited the situation never gave them the legitimacy to say, 'Look what I did,' especially if you were climbing through the coaching ranks. You say, 'Look what I created,' when it was already wrapped up and just handed to you. Well, then you really can't put it on your resume.

"Winning is one thing, but to say you had an integral part in the selection and fielding of certain players, I think that was definitely a factor. I think people had underlying objectives in doing things for themselves.

"Hell, I remember we had media personalities around town, and some are still around, from 1971 and 1972, and these guys were a bunch of nobodies covering what had been a team of nobodies. As we started winning, and whether they were the voice of the team, or wrote a column on the team, they indirectly benefited. And some of the coaches did, too.

Dwight White (78) wasn't happy about his playing time in 1979, when he shared right defensive end with John Banaszak.

Some people used that and manipulated that to their better interest. My point is some people got too smart for their own good. They figured it's not the players. 'It's my great coaching. It's my great ability to handle these guys.' And that was a bunch of bullshit. You had people who wanted to get head coaching jobs and athletic director jobs and they needed to catch a rising star.

"Look at the direction some players and some coaches went as a result of just being on that team. They were able to put down things on their resume that enhanced them. It bothered me, period. Even though it was a great period in Pittsburgh Steeler football history, there were some things from a human resource perspective that probably could've been handled a lot better, from Franco Harris on down."

Harris, of course, rushed for over 1,000 yards in 1983, then held out in 1984 and was unceremoniously released after 12 seasons with the team.

White played through the 1980 season. The two-time Pro Bowler finished his career with 46 sacks.

During the 1979 season, he didn't complain publicly about his playing time being cut in half.

"There was so much winning in the seventies, that if there was something that went down that would absolutely stink, who was going to rock the boat? You couldn't get the media to give a straight story, an objective story on something, because, with all respect to you, hell, the writers at that point were too busy vying for position in the little Steeler kitchenette and they've got celebrity status on the plane. They're protecting that bullshit. So if there was an objective story that needed to be done, it wouldn't have happened because Vito Stellino's worried if he's going to get his feet on the plane. That's just my opinion.

"Hey, after a couple Super Bowls they were signing rookies just for Steeler watches. People just wanted to be on the team so bad they'd sign for a damn watch. That kind of atti-

The NFL abolished contact in coverage after five yards in 1978, but it didn't affect the play of Mel Blount.

tude kind of manifested itself throughout the whole operation. People got egos bigger probably than they should've had and made decisions and judgments based on 'Look at me. I'm great. We're the best thing since canned peaches.' And there were a lot of people who were non-players who dealt with that and manipulated that and benefited from that.

"But, again, when you're winning, and there's an ugly situation, somebody put a turd in the punch bowl, you just sweep it under the carpet and cover it up and keep on going because you don't want to rock the boat."

LEGISLATION

Chuck Noll was asked what the Steelers of the 1970s would be remembered for most.

"A lot of legislation," he answered.

The league, prior to 1978, began allowing more offensive holding. They also took away contact by the pass defenders after five yards. It was designed to take away the style of play favored by Mel Blount, Ron Johnson and Donnie Shell. Add J.T. Thomas to the mix, since the former physical corner had become the physical free safety by the end of 1979, and the entire Steelers secondary had to change its style.

Obviously, they weren't hurt too badly.

"It's about speed and technique," said Blount. "It's about teaching these guys how to move their feet and how to get to the receiver and where to get them. If you're jamming a guy on the side, all you're doing is pushing him into his pattern. But if you're in his chest, you've got more control over him."

"I don't think the rule change hurt Mel as much as people think," said Mike Wagner. "Mel was so big and strong that if he had to jam he could control that receiver and then he was fast enough that he could play man coverage if he had to run with him."

So the rules didn't affect the Steelers.

"They affected everybody," Blount said. "But we had the ability to adjust."

"The theory," Wagner said, "was that the rules had changed to slow down or stop the Steelers' style of defense, particularly our cover-two where we would jam receivers and kind of play this umbrella defense and put the big pass-rush on. It was making it easier to throw the ball. It was harder on our defense, but it was just a blessing for our offense. We had great offensive players and they took advantage of it."

PLAY IT AGAIN, L.C.

L.C., do you remember your four and a half sacks when you beat Cleveland in overtime in '79?

"It's tough to say with these Cleveland games, they were all dogfights. Was that Cody Risien's rookie year?"

Yes.

"Well, he got hurt or something. I was just all over, all in the backfield, all over Sipe the whole game. So they brought the other tackle from the other side over to my side. What was his name? He played over Dwight. Nobody liked him. He was a dirty player. Um, what's his name?"

Dieken?

"Dieken. Yeah. Doug Dieken. They brought him over there. When he came over, after I realized it was him, I said, 'The stuff you got away with on the other side, don't bring that over here 'cause I'm not going to put up with it.' After a few plays they found that wasn't going to work so they moved him back over."

What are your views on losing the team's career sack record in 2003 to Jason Gildon?

"My feeling is it's kind of sad that he breaks the record and gets cut the next year. But going into the season I knew he was going to do it. I just couldn't figure out why it took him half the year to do that. He only needed two or something and didn't get it done until the season was well on its way. And I mean it's not like he really hit the guy or brought the guy down, it was just little fluke stuff. Sacks should be when you put your head on a guy and you slam him to the ground. That's what they should call a sack. Then, too, my thing there is they waited all these years before they started recording the sacks."

Did you miss out on sacks because of the record keeping?

"Oh, no question. I lost quite a few. It was just the time that I played. Regardless, records are going to be broken. We can't get bent out of shape over holding a record. That's for you guys, the reporters, to make a big deal out of to keep fan interest and let the fans know what's going on with the current players."

Are players treated too softly today?

"They don't hit enough for one thing. We on the line hit Wednesday, Thursday and Friday. The lines were pretty much always live. It was the right way to go, especially if an offensive lineman needed to get the feel of a good pass rusher for Sunday. A lot of guys need the real thing."

Thanks, L.C Hope you end up in Canton.

"Well, you know what? One way or another I'm going to end up there. That's where I was born, Canton, Mississippi, so my mother has my plot already paid for. One way or another I'm going to end up there. It might not be Ohio, but I'm going to end up in Canton."

CHAPTER VII

OFFENSE EMERGES:
THE READY-FOR-PRIME-TIME PLAYERS

"Hey, they're laughing at us. Let's go."

—Washington Redskins defensive player

MUST-SEE TV

Only two teams in NFL history have sent four starters at offensive skill positions to the Hall of Fame. The Steelers, of course, sent Terry Bradshaw, Franco Harris, Lynn Swann and John Stallworth to Canton. They played together from 1974 to 1982.

The Baltimore Colts also had four, but didn't win a championship during the five years (1963-67) quarterback Johnny Unitas, running back Lenny Moore, wide receiver Ray Berry and tight end John Mackey played together.

Only two other teams placed receiving duos in the Hall of Fame, but the Washington Redskins didn't even finish above .500 during the five-year (1964-68) heyday of Bobby Mitchell and Charley Taylor.

You'd have to go back to the 1951 NFL champions, the Los Angeles Rams, with Hall of Fame receivers Tom Fears and Crazylegs Hirsch, to find a mix resembling that of the 1979 Pittsburgh Steelers.

While the above research—as well as the 1974, 1975 and 1978 Steelers—might prove defense does indeed win championships, offense put the Steelers over the top in 1979.

"We won that year on the strength of our offense," admitted Joe Greene.

"Well, they changed the rules now," said Bradshaw. "Also, it's like anything else, our team evolved, and as progression had it, I got better. And with Swannie and Stalls, we really became, offensively, pretty dominating. When they took away the bump-and-run, we took advantage of it. You take two great receivers, get 'em past five yards and here we go. We had a great offensive line so we took advantage of it."

It was the beginning of a new era of offensive football, and the '79 Steelers paved the way for Don Coryell and his San

Diego Chargers, and for Bill Walsh and his devotees of the West Coast offense.

To counter the new rules, the Steelers not only opened up their offense, they began blitzing more on defense. But instead of relying on the hunch blitzing Andy Russell had made popular, teams such as the Steelers began playing more zone behind the orchestrated chaos up front.

Then along came Lawrence Taylor and the new breed of linebacker, and defensive coordinators such as Buddy Ryan of the Bears, and blitzing became an art form.

In the late 1980s, Dick LeBeau began dropping linemen into coverage and sending cornerbacks, and the Steelers of the 1990s hired him to refine his "zone blitzes."

It all began with Commissioner Pete Rozelle's attempt in 1978 to bring parity to the league by legislating the Steelers back to the pack. It worked, but only because of poor drafting and Bradshaw's arm problems in the early 1980s.

"If he didn't get hurt there in the eighties, he would've gone on to break all kinds of passing records," Mike Wagner said in 2004. "I was really stunned when watching the '78 Super Bowl highlights this past year, when they announced that was the first time Bradshaw had passed for over 300 yards. It was really a change of trends and Terry was able to do it."

Bradshaw passed for 318 yards against Dallas in Super Bowl XIII. It signaled a change in the way Steelers won football games. The Steelers passed for 965 more yards in 1979 than they did in 1978.

"The rules changes were for television," said Bradshaw, now a pregame host for Fox. "The competition committee looked at the old AFL. There was no defense. It was like the Arena League, throwing that sucker down the field, I mean scoring a lot of points, and the fans were staying tuned. They were having fun.

"In the early seventies if you threw for 200 yards as a quarterback, you, my friend, were on the cover of *Sports Illustrated*.

That's how hard it was against really good bump and run. But it was changed strictly for television and the ratings. 'Let's get 'em off, let's let these little bitty, receivers run down through there and let's get that ball in the air, score more points and let's get ratings up.' So it was all done for television.

"Most of your rules today are done for television. The rule they made off of me getting hurt in Cleveland with my neck was, 'Oh, my God we can't lose our star quarterbacks.' It wasn't, 'He may never walk again.' It was, 'It hurt the league! It's bad for ratings!' Honest to God, everything is driven by TV."

STRONG AS A BULL, SMART AS A WHIP

Of the nine Steelers in the Hall of Fame from the 1970s, five played offense. Center Mike Webster was the fifth.

He didn't begin playing football on offense. He was a defensive tackle in high school, but in his very first game, on an interception return, Webster knocked two guys down with one block. The coaches saw it on film and a Hall of Fame center was born.

Webster was one of three Hall of Fame offensive players drafted by the Steelers in 1974, and Webster, Lynn Swann and John Stallworth, along with classmate Jack Lambert, began entering their prime years in 1979.

Webster's best game that season—or at least the one in which he received the most publicity—was the 10th game. In a 38-7 drubbing of the Washington Redskins, Bradshaw's head was bounced off the Three Rivers Stadium turf by a defensive lineman. His pass was intercepted and as the offense left the field Webster looked at his quarterback and knew something was wrong. He told Chuck Noll about it.

Before Bradshaw could be examined, though, the Redskins fumbled and the Steelers took over at the Washington 4. On the first play, Bradshaw flipped a touchdown pass to tight end Randy Grossman. It gave the Steelers a 24-7 lead with 38 seconds left in the half and it was taken as a sign that all was well with Bradshaw.

In the locker room at halftime, Webster noticed Bradshaw was still woozy. "Then in the second half," Webster said later, "he was still a little dazed."

Webster noticed Bradshaw struggling in the huddle, "like when you can't remember a name. You know what it is but you can't say it." So Webster commenced calling the plays. He called three running plays and then a pass to Stallworth. It was a wobbly pass from a woozy quarterback but it went 65 yards for a touchdown.

It was Stallworth's sixth catch of the game and gave him 126 yards and the team a 31-7 lead, so he took a seat on the bench to rest a sore hamstring. Bradshaw was finished for the day as well. Webster, of course, gave way in the huddle to backup quarterback Mike Kruczek, who closed out the win.

With 311 yards and four touchdown passes, Bradshaw established career regular-season highs, and he did so in only 32 minutes of action.

"If he throws that way dingy," Noll said to Webster, "we ought to keep him dingy all the time."

CATCHING FIRE

The movers and shakers in the Steelers' passing game figured Super Bowl XIII was a turning point, but through the first five games of the 1979 season the Steelers couldn't pass for more than 235 yards. In five games, the Steelers passed for more than 200 yards only twice.

"We're still feeling each other out," reasoned Randy Grossman. "It's going to take some time."

"I know it will start clicking like it did last year," said John Stallworth. "We can't let ourselves down. It'll come."

With tight end Bennie Cunningham out with an injury, Tom Moore began experimenting with three-receiver sets in a 42-7 win over Denver in Week 8 and the offense began to click. Jimmy Smith caught five passes for 55 yards in the Steelers' second 500-yard offensive performance in three weeks. Terry Bradshaw passed for 267 yards.

The Steelers followed with a physical 14-3 win over the Dallas Cowboys, and then came the easy win over the Washington Redskins that marked the Steelers' third 500-yard offensive performance of the season.

The Redskins came into the game with the NFL's stingiest defense statistically, but made the mistake of daring the Steelers to beat them with their passing game. Former Houston Oilers coordinator Richie Pettibon, in going back to a two-year-old win, brought the Redskins free safety up to stop the run with nine players at the line of scrimmage. The Steelers passed them silly.

"I was hemmed in and couldn't go anywhere," Stallworth explained about a second-quarter pass near the Redskins bench, "so I just started laughing as they converged on me. I heard one of the Redskins' say, 'Hey, they're laughing at us. Let's go.' We were on the opposite sides of the scale. I was having a good time and they were all so intense."

The Steelers improved to 9-2 by squashing the Kansas City Chiefs, 30-3. Bradshaw passed for 232 yards with three touchdown passes and two interceptions. The offense had been playing so well that Bradshaw actually believed it when he called it "the worst game I've played all year."

It may have been a premonition of sorts because Bradshaw played his worst game the following week. He threw five interceptions as the visiting Steelers lost to the San Diego Chargers, 35-7.

The Chargers didn't follow the Redskins' formula for stopping the Steelers. Quite the opposite, the Chargers dropped their linebackers deep to double the wide receivers. It foreshadowed game plans to come.

THE GREATEST GAME?

Larry Anderson averaged 25.1 yards per kickoff return as a rookie in 1978, but he was averaging only 21.4 when his slump in 1979 took a turn for the worst. He was benched after fumbling the game's second kickoff against the Cleveland Browns, and the gift field goal gave the Browns a 10-0 lead before the Steelers had run one offensive play.

It was the best game plan the Browns could've devised since in the previous meeting the Steelers had rushed for 361 yards, still a franchise record.

With the early lead, the Browns could play the run loosely and copy the blueprint laid down by the San Diego Chargers. The Browns dropped their linebackers to make it tough on Lynn Swann and John Stallworth, and forced the Steelers to beat them with a banged-up offensive line working once again without left tackle Jon Kolb and right guard Moon Mullins.

The Steelers chipped away with a pair of Matt Bahr field goals, and Terry Bradshaw's two-yard touchdown pass to Franco Harris with 28 seconds left in the half shaved the Browns' lead to 20-13 at the break.

Matt Bahr (9) is hugged by holder Craig Colquitt after kicking a 37-yard field goal with nine seconds left in overtime to beat the Browns, 33-30.

Quarterback Brian Sipe led the Browns to a touchdown to open the second half, but another short Harris touchdown run again cut the Browns' lead to seven, 27-20 entering the fourth quarter.

Don Cockroft kicked his third field goal 5:16 into the final quarter to give the Browns a 30-20 lead, but the Steelers embarked on another long drive leading to another short Harris touchdown run.

Harris then led the Steelers to the tying field goal with 24 seconds remaining. The Steelers won in overtime on Bahr's fourth field goal, a 37-yarder with nine seconds left to play.

While Bradshaw passed for a career-high 364 yards, Harris was the star of the game. He didn't have a run longer than 11 yards but he carried 32 times for 151 yards and caught nine passes for 81 yards.

In taking what the Browns gave them, Harris helped the Steelers rack up 36 first downs, a team record to this day. They also piled up a season-high 606 yards of total offense.

"It was nothing but long drives," Harris said after the game. "That takes a lot out of you."

Livingston, the sports editor of the *Pittsburgh Press*, penned a column under the title "Finest Game Played Here."

Ketchman of the *Standard Observer* wrote, "I've never seen a greater game."

Was Chuck Noll excited?

"Excitement to me is being ahead by a hundred," he said.

The players were too exhausted to be excited.

"The mighty Steelers and all that garbage," said Bradshaw, "let it die."

INTO THE BLACK

Terry Bradshaw not only won the MVP of Super Bowl XIII, he'd won the respect of one Thomas "Hollywood" Henderson.

"Bradshaw is the best quarterback," said the man who'd spotted him the "c" and the "a" and dared him to come up with the "t" before the game.

"I underrated his intelligence, but not his ability," Henderson said.

But the trophy and the ring and the newfound respect of his most critical opponent to his most critical head coach left nothing but emptiness inside Bradshaw.

Signs of depression were evident throughout the 1979 season. Always eager to please, Bradshaw wasn't even pleased with what he saw in the mirror. He wore a toupee for his photo in the media guide, grew a beard early in the season, shaved the beard, grew a mustache in the middle of the season, shaved the mustache. He even took to smoking a pipe in order to look "more intellectual."

On the field he was up and down. He set a team record with four touchdown passes against Washington; he set a team record by throwing five interceptions against San Diego. He would finish the season with a TD-to-interception ratio of 26 to 24. Both numbers still rank second in team history.

Against Cleveland, Chuck Noll excoriated Bradshaw during the game for taking a sack after the Steelers had a late first and goal at the two-yard line. Afterwards, Noll praised his quarterback for doing "an outstanding job of getting the ball to the right person."

It was his third 300-yard game on the way to a record-setting yardage total, *Sports Illustrated* Sportsman of the Year award and second Super Bowl MVP trophy, but Bradshaw felt little joy.

"This is the toughest season I've encountered in my nine years in the league," he told the *McKeesport Daily News* after the second win over the Browns.

The Steelers were 10-3 at the time and tied for first place in the division with the Houston Oilers.

"It's a combination of things that I've allowed to get me down," he said. "I was hearin' rumors that me and Jo Jo (wife Jo Jo Starbuck) are havin' troubles. It's not true, but still it bugs me to hear the talk." Bradshaw also complained about autograph seekers, boo birds and his demanding coach.

A quarter-century later, Bradshaw talked about his struggles with clinical depression.

"I honestly don't think it affected my performance on the field," he said. "When you look back on it, I can pinpoint a lot of instances where depression played a large part in my behavior, but you could also say that due to bad performance, bad relationships, that had a lot to do with sending me deeper into the hole. But also the depression, for me, was a motivating factor.

"One of the things about being depressed, clinically depressed, is it doesn't keep you from seeking and pursuing goals and trying to accomplish things because you need to do that. You say to yourself, 'Boy, if I can win another Super Bowl then that's really going to put me over and I'm going to feel good.' And it never did that, so it was a driving force behind accomplishing things, because you're always pursuing stuff, hoping this is the answer, or this is the answer, and nothing ever is. And while you're doing that, you're accomplishing a lot of wonderful things. So it doesn't prohibit you from being successful. It prohibits you from being happy and being able to enjoy your success."

Bradshaw's struggle led him through three divorces and alcoholism before he visited a preacher in 1999. He told Bradshaw it was not a spiritual issue and directed him to a psychologist, who confirmed what the preacher had said and sent

Bradshaw to a psychiatrist. Bradshaw now takes an anti-depressant to control his mood. He's continued giving motivational speeches throughout.

"I speak to major corporations," he said, "and one of the clauses now in the contract is 'Please don't talk about your mental illness.' So I don't. It's kind of hard to be giving motivational talks and then going, 'By the way, I'm clinically depressed. How do you all feel?' So I don't bring it up."

Bradshaw, with Noll at his side prior to a banquet in Pittsburgh, was asked if Steelers fans had anything to do with the condition.

"Nah," he said with a laugh. "You could probably say 'yes,' but a disease is a disease. A mental illness is a mental illness. Now, it can be triggered by stress and trauma, and if you play a bad game out there on the football field, then you've got to face him (Noll), which is not bad, not bad."

"Blame it all on Turkey Jones," said Noll.

VOODOO LADY; HOODOO MAN

Sidney Thornton sprained his left ankle against the Washington Redskins and missed the next five games, but it was the right ankle he was soaking in a disgusting foamy green mix of ammonia, alcohol and urine in the locker room prior to the December 2 home game against the Cincinnati Bengals.

Thornton had gone home to Dulac, Louisiana, to visit a healer, Miss Rudolph, whom he described as "a thousand years old."

A friend of the family, Miss Rudolph recommended Thornton soak his healthy foot in order to heal his injured

Franco Harris (32) runs away from the Dallas Cowboys and eventually into the record book. His 1,186 rushing yards in 1979 tied Jim Brown's record of seven consecutive 1,000-yard seasons.

foot. Thornton complied, and said he felt better, but didn't play.

Franco Harris did. His early 34-yard run to the 5-yard line brought bad luck to the Bengals in an easy 37-17 win.

It was a game quarterback Terry Bradshaw designated as Lynn Swann Appreciation Day, so Harris didn't receive much more work. He finished with 92 yards on 20 carries and crossed the 1,000-yard mark for the seventh consecutive season to tie a record held by Jim Brown. Harris also passed Joe Perry to become the fourth all-time leading rusher in NFL history with 8,404 yards.

"Franco's a great back," Bengals owner Paul Brown told Livingston of the *Press*. "He's been one for a long time. He's one of those unusual runners who don't come along every day."

Livingston was an historian of the game, so he'd moved over in the press box to interview Brown. He asked Brown to compare Harris to some of the great backs he'd coached in Cleveland.

"There's a jiggle to him, so he's not like Jimmy Brown at all," Paul Brown said. "He doesn't have Brown's power or straight-ahead speed. Brown would take the ball and go. Franco's different. He gets to the same place but he does it in a different way. They're hard to compare.

"(Marion) Motley could do it all—run, block and he played linebacker. He was a great defensive player as well as a great offensive player."

Brown's attention shifted as Swann reeled in yet another catch.

"They're killing our cornerbacks," Brown said to effectively end the interview.

POLITICKING FOR THE BALL

It's been said that Frank Lewis might've had more talent than either Lynn Swann or John Stallworth, but he was too shy to compete for Terry Bradshaw's attention.

"That's a very good observation," said Randy Grossman. "Frank was a No. 1 also, a tremendously skilled guy and physically perhaps as good as Lynn and John. He was not a very good politician. He was just a quiet and shy guy. Whose observation was that?"

Bill Nunn's.

"Oh, yeah. Bill knows talent."

Lewis went on to average 45 catches and 773 yards per his six seasons (including one strike-shortened season) in Buffalo after the Steelers practically gave him away in 1978. With the Bills, Lewis didn't need to lobby for the ball.

"Well," Grossman said, "that was a much more normal situation, where you have a dominant receiver—A dominant receiver. We were fortunate, I guess, that we weren't a normal team. We had amazing talent everywhere."

Johnny Unitas didn't have to worry as much with the Baltimore Colts. Tight end John Mackey was simply a luxury used to surprise defenses when the run-pass combo of Lenny Moore and Ray Berry needed a changeup. Bradshaw used his tight ends similarly, but had two Hall of Fame receivers to keep happy, not to mention the run-oriented coach.

"Everybody politicks for the ball. Nobody wants to block," Grossman said. "With John and Lynn, it was not a personal thing, it was a professional thing. They were open, they want the ball, but there's only one ball."

Stallworth knew he wasn't leading in any of the polls his first three years in the league. He'd been drafted fourth and Swann first. After three seasons, Swann had 88 receptions and

Stallworth had 45. But Stallworth knew he was good, so he went to wide receivers coach Lionel Taylor for advice.

"If you want the ball more, you have to be in Terry's face all the time," Taylor told him. "In the locker room, you've got to be there talking to him. You can't just hang out at your locker and expect to get the ball."

So Stallworth became Bradshaw's shadow.

"All of the sudden," Grossman said, "Lynn realized it and then Terry had two shadows. Where Terry went, they were there.

"All things being equal on the field, who do you think about? You think about the guy you always see."

Taylor left to become, in effect, offensive coordinator of the Los Angeles Rams in 1977. He was replaced by Tom Moore in Pittsburgh and the reveiving stats began to even out. From 1977-79, Stallworth caught 155 passes and Swann caught 152.

Moore, now the Indianapolis Colts' offensive coordinator, realized the competition was healthy. "They both tried to get open and worked very hard to get open and they both wanted every single pass. That's the way great receivers are."

But...

"But they never jumped out of the WE concept," Moore said. "Both of them were tremendous professionals. I think the whole thing was put in a nutshell when Swann was inducted into the Hall of Fame. It was a statement he made, like it's only 50 percent, but it'll be 100 percent when John's here with me. That kind of typified the whole situation."

When Swann was inducted into the Hall of Fame in 2001, he said in his acceptance speech, "If this is the greatest hour of my life, then this is only a half hour. It'll be the greatest hour when I can sit back in that room and John Stallworth is wearing a gold jacket making this speech."

The vision came true the following year.

LYNN'S TURN

To raise money for the Mel Blount Youth Home in 2004, most of the players came together in Pittsburgh to roast Terry Bradshaw, who in turn roasted Lynn Swann.

"Of course, Lynn was always open," Bradshaw said from the podium. "Right, John? Always open. You noticed he didn't show up tonight. Home lookin' at his highlight tape I bet."

Stallworth put the heat back on Bradshaw where it was meant to be.

"They think Terry had a neck problem," Stallworth said. "It forced him to look to his right all the time instead of to the left where I was ... roaming free ... wide open ... miles away from any defensive back."

That "neck problem" surfaced on the first Sunday in December, 1979 when Swann caught five passes for 192 yards and two touchdowns in a romp over the Cincinnati Bengals. Stallworth caught two passes for 18 yards, but wasn't upset.

"I can understand what Lynn has been going through this year, being the No. 2 guy," Stallworth said after the game.

Swann had indeed become second to Stallworth in the pecking order in 1979, and Bradshaw went into the game looking to salve any wounds.

"I wanted to prove that Lynn Swann is back and that he's dangerous," said Bradshaw. "He'll have to be reckoned with."

Swann's troubles began with his three-week "retirement" during training camp when he and three others sued the City of San Francisco over a 1974 incident. Swann was eventually awarded a split of $162,000, which made him "very happy", but he returned to camp and promptly collided with a goal post at full speed. Just as he began to recover, he pulled a hamstring. Swann barely avoided injury in the second Cleveland game when he had to leap over one of the cars parked behind the end zone at Three Rivers Stadium in an attempt to catch an overthrown pass. Swann finally emerged against the Bengals with what would stand as a career-high yardage performance.

"John Stallworth is having a great year, and I hope he understands I have to get Swann back," Bradshaw said after the game.

Of course Stallworth understood.

"He needed a day like this to regain his confidence," Stallworth said.

Chuck Noll's reaction to these warm and fuzzies?

"I have no thoughts about that," he said. "We have to beat Houston next week, that's all I know."

AIN'T NO BUM

Before the 1978 AFC Championship Game, Houston Oilers Coach Bum Phillips declared war and said he was recalling his ambassador from Pittsburgh. The Steelers won, 34-5.

Nearly a year later, the 10-4 Oilers were coming off an upset loss to the Cleveland Browns and needed to either beat the 11-3 Steelers by 20 points or beat them and hope the Steelers lost the following week to the Buffalo Bills. Since it was a long shot, Phillips took a subdued approach to the game.

"The last time we said we declared war, we had to sue for peace," he told reporters.

When asked how his book was coming along, Phillips said: "Pretty good I guess. It's called *He Ain't No Bum*, but Pittsburgh is trying to write a sequel to it called, *Yes He Is*.'"

That Sunday, the Oilers beat the Steelers, 20-17, behind Earl Campbell's first 100-yard performance in five tries against the Steelers.

The Steelers rallied with a late touchdown, and then Larry Anderson recovered an on-side kick with 1:17 remaining. But it was wrongfully (according to the league less than 12 hours later) overruled by Houston native Willie Spencer, who, game films revealed later in the week, also incorrectly called critical offside and pass interference penalties against Mel Blount.

The Steelers raged against the injustice and blamed the crowd noise for offensive confusion, but what really beat the Steelers was a 69-yard, fourth-quarter touchdown drive by the Oilers, who didn't pass once. They went right at the Steelers with the game on the line, and won.

Campbell finished with 109 yards on 33 carries. He thought he was going to run the ball again when the Oilers reached the Pittsburgh 1-yard line and called timeout with one second left on the clock. Pastorini went to the sideline to check on the required margin of victory for tiebreaking purposes.

On his way back to the huddle, Pastorini was pelted with verbal abuse by Jack Lambert and Joe Greene.

"I'm coming to get you Dan," said Greene.

"I'm going to fall on the ball," said Pastorini.

Lambert continued screaming and pointing.

"Cool it, Jack, It was a mistake," Pastorini said. "I'm going to fall on the ball."

He did.

Lambert and Greene, of course, had more to worry about. Not only was their pride gutted by the Oilers' running game, but their Hall of Fame teammate, Jack Ham, dislocated his ankle during the game. Ham's season, and some believe ultimately his career, was finished.

LINEBACKERS RUNNING AMOK

Perhaps Jack Lambert was attempting to compensate for the loss of Jack Ham, but in the regular-season finale against the Buffalo Bills at Three Rivers Stadium, Lambert became involved in fights with Bills guard Joe DeLamielleure and center Willie Parker. Lambert was called a dirty player by former teammate and Bills running back Mike Collier, and accused by Parker of trying "to gouge my eyes out a couple times."

But the bottom line was Lambert and his wingmen, Robin Cole and Dirt Winston, were the backbone of a 28-0 win over the Bills. They held the Bills to 78 yards rushing, and of course no points, but the linebacker everyone was talking about after the game was Bills rookie Jim Haslett, who spiked Terry Bradshaw in the head after Bradshaw had slid out of bounds and lost his helmet.

Haslett grew up in Pittsburgh and graduated from nearby Indiana University of Pennsylvania. He had "a few hundred people here" to watch, but became vilified by Pittsburgh fans for his actions.

"I don't want to come back here for awhile," he told the *Indiana Gazette* after the game. "I had to stand on the sidelines and hear the fans. I don't want to come back to this place for a while."

With that, a barrage of reporters approached Haslett's locker. He refused to talk and then threatened a photographer. He later phoned the *Pittsburgh Press* to apologize for the incident.

"I was just trying to get away from the bodies," Haslett said. "I didn't know whether to jump over him or what. I started hurdling him, and I just got hit from the side."

While Lambert, Bradshaw and Mike Webster all made public statements in support of Haslett, Chuck Noll did not. "There's no question it was an intentional act," Noll said after reviewing game film. "His stride had a little extra in it. ... He reached out and stepped on him."

In 1997, Haslett was hired to become the Steelers' defensive coordinator. At the press conference announcing the hiring, Haslett was asked about the incident, and he did a 180 from his previous explanation.

"We were losing at the time," he said with a straight face. "Sometimes you've got to take matters into your own hands."

Jim Haslett (55) confronts an official who's about to flag him for kicking Terry Bradshaw in the head. Haslett was ejected from the game, a 28-0 win for the Steelers.

MOST VALUABLE PLAYER

Unbeknownst to John Stallworth at the time, a career-long competition with Lynn Swann had begun in the spring of 1973.

The NFL had just drafted its first player—Oliver Ross—from Alabama A&M, and that was reason enough for Steelers scout Bill Nunn to head south and time the A&M juniors. Stallworth, a native of Tuscaloosa, ran a 4.6 40 for Nunn.

It wasn't great, but it was better than the 4.8 Stallworth would run for scouts as a senior with a hip pointer.

The latter time, of course, didn't deter Nunn.

"The thing that sold me on him," Nunn would say 30 years later, "I went on Thanksgiving Day and saw him play at Alabama A&M against Tennessee State and he caught 13 passes. And at that time, Tennessee State had one of the best black college football teams in the country."

The Steelers had also secured the only known game tape of Stallworth, which director of player personnel Dick Haley promptly "lost" and couldn't pass around to the rest of the league, which was the etiquette of the time. Then, at the Senior Bowl, Stallworth's coaches played him at defensive back as the Steelers breathed a sigh of relief.

The Steelers also liked USC's Swann at the time, and he had run a 4.65 40. The Steelers then received another reading of 4.59, so even though Swann "cheated on the start" of his better run, according to Nunn, the Steelers had difficulty deciding between the two receivers.

Noll wanted to draft Stallworth in the first round, but was talked out of it since the personnel department sensed Stallworth was rated much lower by the rest of the league. Noll shot a look to the scouts that said, "You had better be right."

The Steelers took Swann in the first round, Jack Lambert in the second and sweated out a pick-less third round. As their turn in the fourth round approached, Art Rooney Jr. turned to Haley and said, "If he robbed a bank, I don't want to hear it." And then they got their man.

Because of leg problems, and perhaps his fourth-round status behind Swann, Stallworth didn't move into the lineup on a full-time basis until 1978. He caught 41 passes that season and topped it off with touchdown catches of 28 and 75 yards in the Super Bowl.

Stallworth followed it up by being named team MVP in 1979. He fought through wrist problems—including a broken bone in one—to catch 70 passes. And perhaps the greatest single-game performance of his 14-year career was yet to come that season.

While being inducted into the Hall of Fame in 2002, Stallworth learned he had finally "won" in his competition with Swann. In his presentation speech on the steps of Canton, John Stallworth Jr. said, "When I was five, I was in the Pittsburgh Steelers' locker room waiting for my dad. A reporter came up to me and asked who my favorite football player of all time was. With all the confidence in the world, I said Lynn Swann. Today, I'd like to correct that statement and say that my favorite football player is John Stallworth."

THE RECORD BOOK

The Steelers finished the season with 6,258 yards of total offense, only 31 short of the all-time, all-league record set in 1961 by Houston. The number has since been passed by a number of teams, but remains the all-time Steelers record.

The Steelers also set franchise records for yards passing (3,655), points (416), touchdowns (52), first downs (337), first downs passing (179), passes attempted (492), passes completed (272) and most fumbles (47).

A quarter of a century later, the records for touchdowns and fumbles in a season still stand alongside the yardage record.

John Stallworth also set a team record with 70 receptions and finished the season riding a record streak of 43 consecutive games with a catch. It eventually ended at 67. Terry Bradshaw set team records with 472 attempts, 259 completions and 3,724 yards. His yardage record still stands, as do Matt Bahr's records for extra-point attempts (52) and extra points (50) in a season.

The team single-game records still standing from 1979 are yards rushing (361) in the first game against the Cleveland Browns; first downs (36) and first downs combined (58) in the second game against the Browns; five touchdown passes against the Washington Redskins; most fumbles lost in a game (seven) in the first game against the Cincinnati Bengals; and most punt returns (10) against the Buffalo Bills.

The individual single-game records still in the books are Theo Bell's 10 punt returns against the Bills and Bradshaw's five interceptions against the San Diego Chargers. Bradshaw later matched the record in 1981, as did Mark Malone in 1985.

Perhaps the most impressive records of all are Bell's 10 punt returns and the team's seven lost fumbles. Both single-game records are only one shy of current NFL records.

Franco Harris finished the season with 1,186 yards rushing, his best since gaining 1,246 in 1975. His career total of 8,563 rushing yards left him 34 behind Jim Taylor for third place on the all-time list.

The Steelers had no individual league leaders in 1979, but as a team led the NFL in points and yardage. They allowed the fewest yards in the AFC.

The 12-4 Steelers matched the Chargers with the league's best record, but by virtue of their regular-season victory the Chargers were the AFC's top seed in the playoffs.

Named to the 1979 All-NFL team, as selected by three groups of writers, were Stallworth, Jon Kolb, Mike Webster, Joe Greene, Jack Lambert, Jack Ham and Donnie Shell. Named to the Pro Bowl as starters were Stallworth, Webster, Harris, Greene, Ham, Lambert, Shell and L.C. Greenwood. Bradshaw and Mel Blount were named to the Pro Bowl as reserves, with Lynn Swann being named to the Pro Bowl after another player backed out.

Livingston of the *Press* wrote a column on the offense's niche in NFL history. "I'm not ready to say the Steelers are any better offensively than those fabulous, thrill-a-minute (1951) Rams," Livingston concluded. "Perhaps they might be."

Chapter VIII

Super Bowl:
Fear and Loathing in Pasadena

"Thing? This ain't no thing. This is a Terrible Fucking Towel, buddy, and I'm swingin' it."

—Bob Hice

JOSTLING FOR POSITION

The Denver Broncos put up a valiant effort in losing to the Houston Oilers, 13-7, in the AFC wild-card playoff game. The Broncos knocked Dan Pastorini, Earl Campbell and wide receiver Kenny Burrough out of the game, and probably out of the next one against the San Diego Chargers.

That wasn't good news for the Steelers. With a win over the Miami Dolphins, and a Chargers win over the Oilers, the Steelers would play the AFC Championship Game in San Diego. But Oilers Coach Bum Phillips seemed to have a good sense of where the AFC title game would be played.

"I don't believe the road to the Super Bowl goes through Pittsburgh," said Phillips. "I know it does."

And sure enough, the Oilers, playing without Pastorini and Campbell, shocked the Chargers, 17-14. Defensive back Vernon Perry was the hero. He intercepted Dan Fouts four times and blocked a short field goal.

All the Steelers had to do now was beat the Dolphins at home the next day and they'd host the Oilers, the limping Oilers, at Three Rivers Stadium with a fourth Super Bowl appearance on the line.

SLEEPLESS NIGHT

Mike Webster couldn't sleep. Neither could Joe Greene or Robin Cole.

"I talked to three or four other players and they were nervous like I was," said Greene.

The Dolphins weren't that good. They did have Don Shula. And they did have Bob Griese, but he was benched for

John Stallworth (82) makes one of his six receptions during the Steelers' 34-14 playoff romp over the Dolphins. Stallworth scored the Steelers' second touchdown on a 17-yard pass from Terry Bradshaw.

ineffectiveness in Week 12 before taking his job back. They had the third-ranked defense, but Bob Baumhower and Kim Bokamper, while Pro Bowlers, certainly didn't strike fear into anyone. Their receivers were Nat Moore and Duriel Harris, and their running backs were Delvin Williams and Comeback Player of the Year winner Larry Csonka.

So why the worry?

"Last year we rolled into the playoffs with a lot of confidence, maybe overconfidence," Greene explained to the

Standard Observer. "This year there were a couple big games and we didn't measure up."

So the Steelers took the Dolphins seriously, and clobbered them, 34-14.

"Today we made a pretty good team look less than that," Greene said. "Probably Houston winning did a lot for our psyche."

The Steelers held Csonka to 20 yards and knocked Griese out of the game in favor of Don Strock. Both threw an interception; Terry Bradshaw did not. He threw a 17-yard touchdown pass to John Stallworth and a 20-yard touchdown pass to Lynn Swann and the Steelers left the first quarter with a 20-0 lead. They coasted to the win.

Later that day, the 9-7 Los Angeles Rams upset the Dallas Cowboys, 21-19, and would travel to Tampa Bay for the NFC Championship Game.

One by one, the Steelers' strongest challengers were falling by the wayside.

THAT TIME OF YEAR

Dan Pastorini and Ken Burrough were listed as doubtful for the AFC Championship Game, and Earl Campbell, while admittedly hurting, was expected to play. Their replacements against the Chargers, Gifford Nielson and Rob Carpenter, were also hurting.

The Steelers were hurting as well. Dirt Winston had replaced Jack Ham, the NFL's highest paid defensive player ($230,000), at left outside linebacker, and J.T. Thomas had moved from cornerback to free safety to replace Mike Wagner, who'd undergone hip surgery.

J.T. Thomas (24) is congratulated by Dewayne Woodruff after breaking up a pass against the Dolphins. Thomas, who missed the 1978 season with a blood disorder, started in the Super Bowl following the 1979 season.

The offensive line, a problem since early in training camp, was still in a state of flux. Left tackle Jon Kolb had given way to Ted Peterson, who would make his sixth start, and Steve

Courson would make his ninth start, this time in place of right guard Moon Mullins.

There were also the usual aches and pains: Mike Webster bruised his kidney; Sidney Thornton re-injured his sprained ankle; Lynn Swann strained his hamstring; Sam Davis bruised his shoulder; and Jack Lambert played with a slightly separated right shoulder.

"I can't remember not playing in pain this year," Lambert told reporters.

The Steelers' depth was solid. In addition to Thomas, Winston, Peterson and Courson, Gary Dunn and Dwight White were rotating into the defensive line, Dwayne Woodruff had become the nickel back, Rocky Bleier was standing by, and Jimmy Smith was emerging as a threat. At quarterback, Mike Kruczek had replaced Terry Bradshaw in five games because of injury and mopped up in three others.

"I think the '79 team was the greatest team ever because of that depth," said Winston. "I realize I'm biased, and the veterans might say otherwise, but that team had so much talent from top to bottom it was scary."

"I think one of the real heroes of that season was J.T. Thomas," said Wagner. "I'd played with him a number of years and he was a rock-solid corner for us. He was thrown into playing safety and ended up playing in the Super Bowl on the championship team at safety and God bless him."

TIGHT AS KRAZY GEORGE'S DRUM

Bum Phillips was one funny guy. Asked by Pittsburgh reporters for an appropriate epitaph for his tombstone, Phillips said: "He'd have lived a lot longer if he hadn't had to play Pittsburgh six times in two years."

Not all was laidback and homespun in Houston before the AFC Championship Game. Dan Pastorini threw *Houston Post* reporter Dale Robertson through a trailer door three days before the game. Pastorini hadn't cooperated with Robertson throughout the season and took offense when Robertson quoted Pastorini, on his injury, by way of another reporter.

The tightly wound Oilers jumped out to an early lead when Vernon Perry returned an interception 75 yards for a touchdown. Terry Bradshaw's 25-yard run on third and 14 led to a 21-yard field goal and the first quarter ended with the Oilers ahead by 7-3.

A Houston field goal was answered by a 16-yard Bradshaw touchdown pass to Bennie Cunningham, who beat Perry on the play to tie the score.

Mel Blount recovered a Mike Renfro fumble at midfield and in six plays the Steelers took the lead for good. Bradshaw passed 20 yards to John Stallworth to set the halftime score at 17-10.

The Oilers cut into the lead with a fourth-quarter field goal, but a 39-yard Matt Bahr field goal returned the Steelers' lead to seven points.

The Oilers were on the move late in the fourth quarter, but Blount and Ron Johnson forced a Guido Merkins fumble, which Donnie Shell recovered at the Houston 45. A sensational catch by Rocky Bleier gained 20 yards, and Bleier ran twice for eight yards before scoring from the four-yard line with 54 seconds left to put the game away.

Game balls went to Joe Greene, Loren Toews, Shell and Bleier. Steve Furness also played an exceptional game. Franco Harris was the leading rusher with 85 yards on 21 carries.

After holding the Miami Dolphins to 25 yards rushing the previous week, the Steelers held Earl Campbell to 15 yards on 17 carries. The Oilers gained just 24 yards rushing.

Campbell was helped off the field several times, but wouldn't use his groin injury as an excuse. "I have no effects from the injury," he said after the game.

Phillips also failed to use a controversial call in the end zone as an excuse. Late in the third quarter, with the Steelers leading by 17–10, Pastorini lofted a pass to Renfro, who out—jumped Johnson for the ball and came down, replays indicated, with both feet in bounds. But side judge Donald Orr ruled Renfro, with his back to Orr, was juggling the ball. After a conference, the call stood and the Oilers settled for a field goal.

Television replays during the game couldn't answer the question of possession. The next day, film from an NFL cameraman at ground level showed Renfro catching the ball, but also showed Renfro attempting to secure a better grip as he was stepping out of bounds. The play had been called correctly.

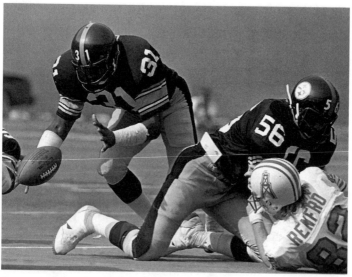

Donnie Shell (31) recovers a fumble as Robin Cole (56) helps with Mike Renfro of the Oilers. The fourth-quarter play led to the last touchdown of the Steelers' 27-13 win in the AFC Championship Game.

"I would've ruled it a catch," said Dirt Winston. "But it wouldn't have mattered. Even if they had scored, we would've dug in. We would've won. We would've found a way; I have no doubt about it."

In Tampa, the Los Angeles Rams blanked the Buccaneers, 9-0, to secure the spot opposite the Steelers in the Super Bowl in Pasadena. Phillips was asked for a prediction on the game.

"I don't think anybody can beat Pittsburgh, except Houston," he said. "And we didn't."

WINDING ROAD BACK HOME

"We went from a 4-5 record to the Super Bowl," said Bad Rad. "Wanna know how we did it?"

Sure.

"The turning point came when we were 4-5," Dan Radakovich, offensive line coach of the Los Angeles Rams, said. "We were in trouble. (Coach Ray) Malavasi was in trouble. I told him I had to talk to him. I told him he'd get fired unless he made some changes. He said, 'What do you mean?' I told him he should change captains and some other things, and he did. (Rich) Saul and Larry Brooks became captains and (Jack) Youngblood stayed a captain, so two on defense and one on offense. Then we went up to play Seattle when we were 4-5 and I had told him I wanted to be in the press box, too. I had been on the field. Then we set the all-time defensive record against Seattle for fewest yards (-7). It's still an all-time NFL record. One of the reasons we did it was offensively we gained over 300 yards rushing and Pat Haden was red hot, completed like 13 in a row and then broke his finger. That's how (quarterback Vince) Ferragamo ended up playing. We won 24-0. It was a total team effort.

"So that started us and of course that wired us up. We went on into the playoffs, made them with a game to go, actually lost the last game. Then we beat Dallas with (Billy) Waddy catching a big pass at the end. We beat Tampa and went to the Super Bowl."

The Betting Line

The Steelers were favored by nine and a half points against the Miami Dolphins and by nine against the Houston Oilers and covered both numbers. So when Bob Martin of the Union Plaza Hotel in Las Vegas set the line at Steelers -10 against the Los Angeles Rams, he wasn't surprised when it jumped quickly to 10.5 and then to 11 by game day. It was the largest spread since Minnesota was favored by 11 over Kansas City in the fourth Super Bowl. The largest spread was Baltimore by 18 over New York in the third Super Bowl.

Both of those favorites lost the game, but that didn't quiet Rams Coach Ray Malavasi, who was furious with the lack of respect shown by Las Vegas, or more precisely the general public.

"People in gambling know a lot more about football than people in football know about gambling," said Martin, who went on to explain his position to the *Post-Gazette*.

"Malavasi's right that his team matches up pretty well with the Steelers. The offensive lines are about equal, and the Rams match up well on defense, especially now that Jack Ham is out. But the Steelers have a far superior quarterback, a decided edge in the wide receivers, and a slight edge in the kicking game."

Why weren't the Steelers favored by more points?

"The Steelers have lost all four on the road, they're playing on grass, and the Rams are the home team, so their home life won't be disrupted, although the Steelers have been through all that before."

THE SCOUTING REPORT

Houston Oilers assistant coach Ed Biles gave a professional advance of the Steelers before Super Bowl XIV in a pool report coordinated by the *New York Times*. These were some of his more interesting points:

- "On second down and long yardage, most teams pass. But not the Steelers. With their great trap blocking, they often will run on such a second down, doing the opposite of what is expected."
- "The Steelers have all but abandoned the I formation. They are saying, 'We're not here to beat you with trickery, like a Dallas. We're here to execute our plays.'"
- "There is a frequency to pass inside the opponent's 30-yard line, and the target would be Lynn Swann."
- "The threat of trap blocking slows down the pass rush. It has almost replaced the draw play and the screen pass as an antidote to the pass rush."
- "One of the most interesting parts of the game (will be) seeing what Ram cornerbacks Pat Thomas and Rod Perry can do with Swann and Stallworth. All four can jump, but who can jump the highest?"
- "In a double-tight-end situation, Grossman will line up as a wingback, then come across and trap block. It doesn't seem fair."

- "(Bradshaw) has great physical abilities but his play-calling is average in that he is not going to come up with any surprises."
- "Bud Carson, Dan Radakovich and Lionel Taylor were Steeler coaches and they know Bradshaw. They will put in some things to try to get him off balance, and when Terry is off balance he can make some mistakes. He is human. Mistakes will keep the Rams in the game."
- "Franco Harris has lost nothing. He can still get outside."
- "The only team that ran against them was the Oilers in the second of their games and Earl Campbell took a terrible beating to get his 100 yards."
- "The Pittsburgh (defensive) line is paying more attention to techniques now than four or five years ago when it was just awesomely physical."
- "It is obvious that Greene is playing better because he is unselfish. He now has the team concept in mind."
- "The Rams' I-formation will not bother Lambert at all."
- "The most physical secondary in the league might have some trouble with (Billy) Waddy."
- "On special teams, the Steelers use a number of regulars, which is something else distinctive about them."

Many of the amateur scouting reports on the Rams focused on the advantage presented by Carson, the Rams defensive coordinator and architect of the great Steel Curtain.

Former Steelers defensive back Tony Dungy, then with the San Francisco 49ers, told of watching Carson throughout the 1979 season and how he'd play a key role in the Super Bowl.

"If anyone can come up with something it's Bud," Dungy said, and he pointed out how the Rams beat the Dallas Cowboys with a new alignment.

"Bud crossed them up. With seven defensive backs, somebody could take Preston Pearson man to man. Usually that's a linebacker and the only linebacker in the league who can cover Preston is Jack Ham. ... This had to be Bud's most satisfying year."

MEDIA DAY

Steelers defensive coordinator Woody Widenhofer didn't take kindly to all of the attention being given Bud Carson.

"This isn't that little architect's defense," Widenhofer snapped. "He didn't know anything about defense until he got with Chuck Noll."

Widenhofer explained how the Steelers had evolved into a complex, blitzing defense since Carson left for the Rams in 1978.

"He's craving a head football job and that's why he left the Steelers," Widenhofer said.

Mel Blount, the Pro Bowl right cornerback, also mentioned Carson on Media Day, but not with the same hostility.

"If they're taking advice from Bud, they'll probably stay away from me," Blount said. "I think he knows what kind of ability I have."

At Media Day prior to Super Bowl IX, Blount had ripped into Carson for yanking him from the AFC Championship Game against Oakland in favor of Jimmy Allen. Carson told Blount after the game he pulled him because he wasn't playing to his potential.

"That was a stupid answer," Blount said before facing the Minnesota Vikings. "I don't think smart coaches would've done something like that."

Blount also said, "If the Vikings' game plan is to throw my way, then they're in trouble."

The remarks before Super Bowl IX sent shock waves through Pittsburgh. Musick, then with the *Press*, wrote Blount "has probably talked himself off the roster if there is a decent cornerback to be had in the draft." In fact, the Steelers did draft cornerback Dave Brown in the first round a few weeks later and lined him up behind Blount on the first day of training camp in 1975.

One year later, Blount was the reigning NFL Defensive Most Valuable Player and Brown was with the expansion Seattle Seahawks, given away for nothing.

Five years later, Blount was making similar statements before a Super Bowl and the reaction in Pittsburgh, after a stifled yawn, was "Give 'em hell, Mel."

Wash Day Hotline

One of the overlooked stories of Media Day was Vince Ferragamo predicting the Rams would win the game. Perhaps the five or six reporters sitting at his table figured he was merely a weak imitation of Joe Namath, since Ferragamo's quote barely drew a mention in the sixth graph of the AP report that day. It made a splash in Pittsburgh, though, thanks to Steelers radio color analyst Myron Cope.

"The interview was proceeding in the typical, uninteresting vein," Cope said 25 years later. "So I said to Ferragamo, 'Have you got any interesting predictions?' And he said, 'Well, the Rams are going to win the game. No doubt about it.' He was very emphatic that the Rams were gonna win. So I left there after nobody picked up on it at the table, which surprised me. You'd think, 'Hey wait, the quarterback flat out predicts victory like Joe Namath did.' But they went on to other topics.

"So I got back to the team hotel and the lobby was packed with Steeler fans as it always was, and I ran into Bradshaw crossing the lobby. So I told him what Ferragamo said. By this time, Bradshaw had won three Super Bowls, and Bradshaw turned absolutely livid. He turned beat red when he heard that, and he said, 'He really said that?' I said, 'Yeah, I asked the question and he said it flat out that they're gonna beat you.' He said, 'Well, we'll see about that.'"

Cope broadcast his talk show back to Pittsburgh later that afternoon. He was set up in an adjoining room to the Steelers' locker room, and his show started just as the players were walking in from the practice field. Over walked Bradshaw, who began shouting, "Here comes the great Vinny Ferragamo. Hey, Cope, you want Dr. Ferragamo on your show?"

Cope picked right up on it and said, "Hey, what are you doing here, Vinny? Sure I want you on the show, doctor."

So Bradshaw sat down with Cope and the two went off on an improvisational jag that mocked the inexperienced Ferragamo and his bold prediction.

"Bradshaw was really pumped up, I'm telling you," Cope said. "He carried that into the ballgame I'll betcha, because when I told him about it, I never saw him livid like that.

"You know, Bradshaw could roll with anything, but here's this punk, who ended up riding the bench in the Canadian League, talking like that."

Cope learned later that his station had received a call from a woman who really thought Bradshaw—who hadn't attempted to disguise his voice—was Ferragamo.

"She was furious," Cope said. "She said, 'I hope the Steelers kill him.'"

THE LONG HAUL

Jerry Finn is better known to Myron Cope's talk-show audience as Zivko Kovalchik from the South Side, but Zivko was working for O'Brien and Gary when he took an imaginary bus trip from Pittsburgh to Los Angeles before the Super Bowl. He made daily reports to the popular morning show and it became an anticipated feature during an otherwise excruciating wait for football fans.

The trip must've sounded like a good idea to Bill Priatko. A friend of Chuck Noll's and a former Steelers player, Priatko packed an RV with 15 friends and drove to Pasadena. Some of the crew ended up on the sideline at practice two days before the game and got the real scoop.

"I was fortunate to have watched the closed workout on Friday," said Priatko. "I distinctly remember that one in '79 because I was standing there talking with Mr. Rooney. Bradshaw's dad was also on the sideline, a nice guy. We had a nice talk. Of course Mr. Rooney was always so congenial. He made everybody feel like you were his favorite person. That's the type of guy he was.

"I talked to Chuck, too. He said when he was coaching with the Chargers he drove from the West coast to the East coast by himself and said it was a long haul. But we had 16 of us, a lot of food, it was a great trip up. It was a great one going back, too.

"The thing I remember from that one, in '79, we were watching the workout, my brother John and I with these guys from Homestead, and the Steelers were going through their defensive sets, running the Ram plays, and they ran a tight end on an eight-yard square in, and George Perles said to Lambert, 'On third and seven, third and eight, look for this, Jack. They like it.' So they ran it in practice and Lambert picked it off. And when the Steelers picked off a pass in practice, they all have an expression they all holler out. So apparently Lambert's nickname was 'Loony' and they all started yelling out, 'Loony.' So I put that in the back of my mind."

The Bar Scene

Dwight White knew the ins and outs.

"When it's not your first time going to the dance," he said, "you've got a little more wiggle room for the extracurricular activities."

So, Dwight, you must have some good stories to tell.

"And you'll never hear 'em from me, dad. Oh, no. Oh, no," White said. "We were all sitting around playing backgammon, taking in the flora and the fauna there on the West coast. We took in flora and fauna a couple times, too."

Jack Lambert didn't tackle the L.A. bar scene, but he wasn't a hermit. Lambert spent his leisure time drinking at the hotel bar with assistant coaches or in the floor above, reported the *Pittsburgh Press*, "dancing to the disco beat"—if anyone can believe that.

Several of Lambert's teammates were more adventuresome. Gary Dunn invaded a bar owned by his former college roommate, Rams starting right guard Dennis Harrah. Dunn brought Mike Webster, John Banaszak, Steve Furness, Mike Kruczek and Steve Courson, among others, with him throughout the week.

"If I can keep the Steelers in my restaurant every night until the Super Bowl, we'll win the game," Harrah told reporters.

Harrah might also have gone broke.

"One night I brought the whole defensive line, some of the linebackers, I think even Lambert got out," Dunn said, "and we ate and drank and even messed up a few chairs and did some other stuff and then walked out on the tab. Next day he calls me up, 'Hey, what in the world?' I said, 'Aw, we were just kidding around. I'm getting the guys together and we're going to pitch in for the table.' He said, 'OK, I'll meet you after practice today.'

"So we all got together and threw in a dollar each, so he got about $12 for the tab. After that he got in the papers and just was butchering me and started killing us about how cheap we were. He ended up putting it on the Rams. After they lost the game, they had a party at Legends and he ended up putting it on their tab anyway."

Actually, Harrah did gain a measure of revenge.

"One night later in the week Dennis was driving me back to the hotel," said Dunn, who now owns the Ocean View Tavern in the Florida Keys.

"They didn't have curfew, but we were about five minutes from our curfew and we're pulling up to our fancy hotel in Newport Beach. All the press and everybody was in the lobby, all that stuff's going on. Dennis doesn't have a curfew, but I kept telling him, 'Man, you have to get me back. I've got curfew.' So he goes flying up in front of the hotel and slams on the brakes. I have this beer in my hand and it splattered all over the front of me. Then he jumps out of the car and starts yelling, 'Gary Dunn of the Pittsburgh Steelers is late for curfew!' They started taking pictures. I just crawled into the place."

Repercussions?

"No. Got lucky. Nothing bad came out of it."

STEELER NATION

Gonzo journalist Hunter S. Thompson, writing for ESPN.com in 1999, described fans on the road to Super Bowl XXXV this way: "They are on their way to the Super Bowl & so are the gamblers & the whores & the mass of foul scum they bring with them. A winning team on the road to the Super Bowl is like a traveling circus that picks up more & more fleas at every stop along the way & finally deposits the whole load on an innocent city like Tampa."

Well if the good doctor had wanted to experience honest fan essence, genuine fear and loathing at a Super Bowl, he would've hitched a ride with Bob Hice.

Before scoring tickets to Super Bowl XIV, the greatest moment in Hice's life occurred when a limo pulled up next to him at a stop light and Ronnie Van Zant, singer for Lynyrd Skynyrd, rolled down the window and tossed him a doobie.

But here was Hice, 21, a machinist in the Westmoreland County village of Adamsburg, boarding a plane for Los Angeles with two friends, his mother and stepfather. They'd bought into a great deal right before the Super Bowl. A pilot chartered a plane and sold game tickets and round-trip fare for $250 per person.

With little more than a "Free Form WYDD and The City of Champions" t-shirt on his back and a Terrible Towel in his pocket, Hice set off for the Super Bowl.

"We met at my stepdad's house at six on Sunday morning for a 10:30 flight," he said. "Right away, everyone, except for my mom, started smokin' weed and drinkin'. We're goin' to the Super Bowl, dude."

They drove down Route 30, over the Parkway, through the tunnels and to the airport, singing "We're from the town with the great football team, boom, boom, boom, boom ..."

They checked in and boarded the plane with big smiles on their faces.

"There were a bunch of friends on the plane, and after we buckled up they announced there was an open bar with free Bud and free shots, those little plastic bottles. Free! So we started pounding some more, then we took off and everyone started lightin' up joints. Then some old biker with a lot of money pulled out this mirror and started cutting up big lines of coke. That's when my mom and stepdad moved up to the front of the plane. They kind of disassociated from us."

In '79, Hice was 21 and he called the sky his own.

"That's pretty good. You're a smart guy. But anyway, the pilot's wife was the stewardess. She was a fine lookin' lady. I got my camera out, went into the cockpit, sat in the co-pilot's chair, snapped some pictures of the pilot, the nose of the plane. Then his wife walked in and I went to take her picture and she smiled, but at the last second I aimed down at her tits and clicked the picture. That's when I got shut off. No more free Bud for me. 'Fuck it,' I said. 'I'm goin' to the Super Bowl.'

"We got to LAX, us country boys, and the airport was a city in itself. I was back with my mom and stepdad and wasn't embarrassing anyone, so we all got on the chartered bus. They had banners hung outside the bus and we took off for Pasadena.

"We stopped for lunch somewhere in L.A. and everyone went in to eat, but us three boys with our Steeler shirts and Terrible Towels said, 'Fuck it. Let's go raise hell.' That's when we snorted coke off a sidewalk at noon in L.A. Got pictures of that, too. Didn't have a care in the world. Didn't even look around. We're walkin' around yelling, 'Steelers!' We ran into some Mexicans who hated the Rams and one of them said, 'I hope you kick their asses.' We said, 'Right on.'

"We got back to the restaurant and the bus and here we go to the Rose Bowl. We got there early and it was a huge parking lot. The driver said, 'Now this is where we're at.

Remember this spot. We're leaving at this time and you'd better be here.' We said, 'Yeah, yeah, yeah,' and in we went."

KICKOFF

Tom Brookshier praised the Steelers as "maybe the best tackling team I've ever seen."

His partner on the telecast, Pat Summerall, praised Steelers fans.

"I don't know if the Rams have any more fans here than the Steelers," he said. "They're certainly not more vocal."

A moment of silence was taken for the hostages in Iran, Cheryl Ladd sang the national anthem and the Chief was driven to midfield for the coin toss in the back seat of a 1933 Duesenberg. There he joined his friend Ed Kiely and Steelers captains Sam Davis, Joe Greene and Jack Lambert.

A pumped-up Lambert made two tackles behind the line to open the game. The Steelers took the ball and ran six straight times, and Rocky Bleier was stopped for a loss on the sixth by tackle Larry Brooks.

"Gene Upshaw told me Larry Brooks is the best he's ever faced," said Brookshier.

Terry Bradshaw then passed 32 yards to Franco Harris over the middle. It was a play designed to beat teams dropping their linebackers deep into coverage, as the San Diego Chargers had done, as everyone had done lately, but by now Bradshaw had become more patient and the play led to a 41-yard field goal by Matt Bahr.

Bahr popped up the kickoff in an onsides-type gamble, but the Rams caught it at their 41, and on the first play Wendell Tyler took off for 39 yards over the left side. Left tackle Doug France ran over Dwight White and blocked Lambert, who in turn tripped Greene, while Mel Blount and J.T. Thomas missed tackles and Dirt Winston overran the play. Donnie Shell finally ran Tyler down at the Pittsburgh 14. Six running plays later, Cullen Bryant squeezed in from the 1 to score only the 10th rushing touchdown of the season against the Steelers.

Larry Anderson returned the kickoff to the Pittsburgh 47 and Franco ripped off an 11-yard run thanks to Davis's block on Brooks, the best player in the world on the last series. A 12-yard pass to Lynn Swann put the Steelers at the L.A. 18 as the first quarter ended with the Rams on top 7-3.

The second quarter opened with Bradshaw passing 13 yards to Bennie Cunningham for a first down at the 5. Bradshaw then completed his only pass of the first three quarters to John Stallworth, who brought it down at the 1. Harris took a pitch, gained the corner on Randy Grossman's block and followed Rocky Bleier into the end zone for a touchdown and a 10-7 Steelers lead.

The Rams continued to find success running wide on the Steelers before Vince Ferragamo threw a 10-yard screen pass to Tyler and a 20-yard pass to Lawrence McCutcheon. A questionable pass interference penalty on Shell, in man coverage on the dangerous Billy Waddy, put the ball at the Pittsburgh 18, and Bryant cut back to reach the 10.

On third down, Ron Smith beat Shell but dropped a touchdown pass and the Rams settled for a 31-yard field goal by Frank Corral, who'd missed his previous nine kicks from beyond 30 yards, and the score was 10-10.

Anderson returned the kickoff to the Pittsburgh 45, but the teams exchanged punts. Bradshaw then threw an interception into the chest of strong safety Dave Elmendorf and the Rams took over at the Pittsburgh 39.

On fourth and eight, Ferragamo passed 10 yards to Waddy, who'd beaten Shell. The Rams' offensive game plan at this point had become obvious: Run wide on the young linebackers and isolate Shell, Thomas and Ron Johnson in coverage, or in other words avoid Mel Blount. The Rams advanced to the Pittsburgh 13, but on third and 10 Ferragamo was sacked for a 15-yard loss by John Banaszak.

"They brought everybody but Art Rooney Senior," Brookshier said during the replay. "There's so many coming, the blockers don't even know who to hold."

Corral's 45-yard field goal with 14 seconds left in the half gave the Rams a 13-10 lead. The ensuing return by Anderson went to the Pittsburgh 45, but was brought back because of a penalty.

HALFTIME

Joe Greene didn't look well as he limped down the steps and into the locker room.

There was a kid, about 12 years old, watching closely.

Kid: Mr. Greene. Mr. Greene.

Greene: Yeah.

Kid: You need any help?

Greene: Uh, uh.

Kid: I just want you to know … I think, I think, you're the best ever.

Greene: Yeah, sure.

Kid: You want my Coke? It's OK. You can have it.

Greene: No, no.

Kid: Really, you can have it

Greene: OK (chugs drink).

Kid: See you around.

Greene: Hey, kid, catch (tosses jersey).

Kid: Wow. Thanks, Mean Joe.

In the Evening

Larry Anderson returned the second-half kickoff to the Pittsburgh 39, and on third and two, the Steelers lined up with two tight ends. The Rams brought Nolan Cromwell up to the line and old-school football was at hand. Ten defenders went up against 10 offensive players at the point of attack. Mike Webster and Larry Brown double-teamed tackle Mike Fanning; Moon Mullins trapped Hacksaw Reynolds; and Sam Davis handled Larry Brooks to spring Franco Harris for the first down. Two plays later, Terry Bradshaw lofted a 47-yard touchdown pass to Lynn Swann.

On his jump, Swann's waist rose above the head of cornerback Pat Thomas. Cromwell ran over and timed his leap almost perfectly but missed by inches as Swann caught the ball and landed at the 2 before falling into the end zone. The touchdown gave the Steelers a 17-13 lead with 12:12 left in the third quarter.

The Rams came right back. On third and six, Vince Ferragamo threw a 50-yard bomb to Billy Waddy, who out jumped and outfought Ron Johnson for the ball at the Pittsburgh 24. On the next play, Lawrence McCutcheon took a pitch right, cornerback Johnson came up and McCutcheon lofted a pass to Ron Smith for a touchdown. Frank Corral came back to earth and missed the extra point but the Rams led by 19-17.

The Rams finally stopped Anderson on a return. He was tackled at the Pittsburgh 28, giving him a then-Super Bowl record 162 return yards for the game. After a 14-yard pass over the middle to Franco, Bradshaw took a snap and rolled to his right. He stopped and threw back to the middle of the field. His pass hit the charging Rams safety Cromwell in the chest, but Cromwell dropped it with open field in front of him.

Bradshaw then threw high to Swann, who jumped high above Thomas for the short pass. This time, Thomas drove his helmet forward, flipping Swann onto his head and neck. He left the game and did not return. On the next play, Bradshaw threw into double coverage and was intercepted by nickel back Eddie Brown.

The Steelers had another chance to regain the lead in the third quarter. A 20-yard pass over the middle to Harris and a 22-yard pass to Sidney Thornton put the Steelers at the L.A. 16.

"Kind of a drive," said Tom Brookshier in the booth.

"Kind of a game," said Pat Summerall.

On third and 10, however, Bradshaw threw into double coverage again. Dave Elmendorf tipped the ball into the air and Rod Perry picked it off.

In three quarters of play, Bradshaw had thrown 16 passes, completed 12 to his teammates and three to the Rams. The only ball to hit the ground was the pass Cromwell had dropped.

The Rams' Wendell Tyler ripped off a 13-yard run to conclude the quarter and the Rams sprinted to the other side of the field, clinging to a 19-17 lead and dreaming of the upset.

"They might have set some kind of record getting to the other side of the field, all 11 of them," said Summerall as the fourth quarter began.

And it began on a positive note for the Steelers. Loren Toews and Steve Furness sacked Ferragamo and effectively ended the Rams' possession. They punted, and on third and eight, from the Pittsburgh 27, Bradshaw threw deep to a streaking Stallworth. He ran a hook-and-go past Perry, looked over his left shoulder and caught it over his right, in stride, at the L.A. 30 and sprinted into the end zone for a 73-yard touchdown.

"Over the wrong shoulder!" shouted Brookshier. "That's one of the great catches you'll ever see!"

The teams traded punts before the Rams started to drive from their own 16, trailing 24-19, with 8:29 remaining.

The Steelers dropped into a three-deep zone and Preston Dennard cut over the middle, as Mel Blount backpedaled, and caught a 24-yard pass. Blount showed his disdain on the next play. Dennard ran a hitch in front of Blount, who shifted out of his backpedal quickly this time and lifted the pass-catcher before dropping him on his head at the L.A. 49. Rams trainers ran onto the field with smelling salts, averting what today would be a 15-minute break for corporate America. Dennard was dragged off the field, replaced by Smith, and play resumed.

The Rams crossed midfield with 7:09 left, but Dwight White tackled Tyler for a three-yard loss, and an incomplete pass brought up third and 13. The Steelers had declined offsides on the play, and were burned when Waddy caught a 14-yard pass over nickel back Dwayne Woodruff for a first down at the Pittsburgh 32 with 5:35 left.

On the next play, Ferragamo passed to Smith running a down-and-in and the ball was intercepted by Jack Lambert at the 14. He returned it to the Pittsburgh 30 with 5:24 left.

"Smith, coming across, sort of drifting," explained Brookshier as the Steelers' biggest defensive play of the season was being replayed. "I don't think he was supposed to pull up like that. He was supposed to either clear out that zone or keep moving across. He died on the pattern." Smith's coaches would agree with Brookshier later in the locker room.

The Steelers ran the ball a couple times and on third and seven, Bradshaw called signals as the clock rolled under 4:00. He dropped back and with plenty of time threw another bomb to Stallworth, who was behind Perry and Elmendorf again and looking back over his left shoulder. Stallworth slowed down, bent back, back, back to his right and squeezed the ball against his facemask as he fell on his back at the L.A. 22.

It was a 45-yard completion on the exact same play—a hook-and-go out of the slot with Jimmy Smith and Bennie Cunningham split wide—which had given the Steelers their lead earlier in the quarter.

"OK. OK, John. That tops the last one," announced Brookshier with resignation in his voice. "He's not going to believe it when he sees this replay, either."

A questionable interference call against Thomas on a pass in the end zone to Smith moved the Steelers to the 1, and from there Harris scored to put the game away, 31-19.

IN THE LOCKER ROOM

Joe Greene: "This game was an invitation engraved in gold." An invitation to what? "To immortality."

John Stallworth: "I've made better catches in Super Bowls, a couple of one-handers one time."

Terry Bradshaw on the same-play bombs to Stallworth: "I didn't like the call but, you know, the coach sent it in."

Chuck Noll: "We tried to go deep as often as we could to get the big play because we knew they would take away the high-percentage passes."

Mike Webster on the dropped interception by Nolan Cromwell: "The only thing that could've stopped him was a .357 magnum."

Steelers defensive coordinator Woody Widenhofer: "We were waiting for them to throw that in route all day. The first time they did, Jack jumped on it."

Jack Ham: "I'm not taking anything away from (MVP) Bradshaw, but I thought Lambert was the best player on the field until Stallworth made those big catches at the end."

Rams cornerback Rod Perry: "I did the best I could. Hey, haven't you ever seen a perfect play?"

The CBS-TV crew, of course, had first dibs on the locker room. A young Brent Musberger, mixing up the local baseball team's disco slogan with the shot-and-beer football crowd, struck first.

Musberger: "We are Fam-a-lee indeed! And for the fourth time the Rooneys and the Pittsburgh Steelers have won the Super Bowl. It is my pleasure to introduce Commissioner Pete Rozelle to make the award presentation."

Rozelle: "Mr. Rooney, we'll have to stop meeting like this. I think it's absolutely incredible. Your team was tested by an outstanding Rams club and your team came back every time. I know for you it had to be particularly rewarding to have your son, Danny, president of the club, play a part in this win for the franchise, which you started 46 years ago. I know for you, the big thrill was being able to deliver to the City of Champions, your beloved Pittsburgh, this trophy."

As the beaming Chief held the Lombardi Trophy, the players began chanting, "Speech! Speech! Speech!" And Musberger promptly blundered. He stretched the microphone across the small stage, past the Chief, and said, "Coach Noll, I think your players want you to speak now!"

The bobbing and nodding and grinning Musberger continued to interview Noll for a seeming eternity as the Chief stood in the middle of the two without ever having said a word.

In the Radio Booth

"It was a pity Ham couldn't play, and who knows how the game would've been affected," said Myron Cope. "Probably, the Steelers might have won more easily because Ham was a Hall of Fame linebacker. He sat in our broadcast booth for the kickoff. It was a makeshift booth, an out-of-the-way booth we always got at the Super Bowl, somewhere down near the end zone. It was a spacious booth, no beefs about the booth, but next door to us was the Japanese radio crew and they had a much smaller booth. They had a crew of about 40 people squeezed into there. They couldn't have all been working because one by one they started drifting into our booth. Finally, we got about five Japanese in there and it was crowded. Well, I blew my top. I said, 'What the hell is this, Pearl Harbor?' (Jack) Fleming nearly collapsed. Fleming could hardly broadcast the next few plays, he was laughing so hard.

"He always mentioned that, for years after, 'What the hell is this, Pearl Harbor?'

"And I yelled for a security guy who was luckily standing outside. I said, 'Get these guys outta here. They've got no business in here.' So the security guy ordered them out. I don't know how it affected our relations with Japan. He cleared them out."

IN THE HUDDLE

Franco Harris rushed for only 46 yards on 20 carries, his low in four Super Bowls. The Steelers as a team rushed for only 84 yards, but it wasn't for lack of trying. Their plan coming in was to double-team the Rams' stout left defensive end Jack Youngblood and to trap the Rams' pass-rushing right end Fred Dryer. But Terry Bradshaw kept confusing the sides. When reminded in the huddle he was calling the running plays backwards, Bradshaw would reply, "Shut up. This is my huddle."

The Steelers' defense, meanwhile, was sluggish, particularly in the first half. Joe Greene admitted after the game he "wasn't 100 percent into it" in the first half. It was quite the topic at halftime.

"Lambert was really the one who got us into it," said Gary Dunn. "We were kind of flat in that game for some reason. In the second half, man, he started yelling at everybody, saying, 'What's a matter with ya? Everybody's dead out here.' And we were. We were just kind of flat. And after he got in the huddle and started screaming at everybody and saying, 'Let's make something happen,' he backed it up with the big interception."

On the Sidelines

Several offensive players believed the Rams had an understanding of their offensive audible system. And Steelers defensive play-caller George Perles believed his counterparts with the Rams, former coaching mates Bud Carson, Dan Radakovich and Lionel Taylor, even knew his play-calling signals.

Perles called it "a chess game" and said, "I didn't have to be sharp to realize what was going on. I picked it right up after a couple of plays." So Perles had linebackers Loren Toews and Robin Cole shuttle plays.

Carson laughed about it 25 years later. "That was all bullshit from Perles. Nobody knew the calls. I just thought we matched up with them well. We had the right defense to handle Pittsburgh I thought. We had an odd stack-over type defense that we played a lot. The year before we beat Pittsburgh in Los Angeles. They had a hard time with that, a real hard time. I don't think they got 200 yards on us."

On November 12, 1978 the Rams held the Steelers to 174 yards of total offense in a 10-7 win. It was the Steelers' last loss of the 1978 season.

"Once Lynn Swann went out of the game it wasn't very hard to imagine him throwing the ball a lot to Stallworth," Carson said. "We set it up so that we doubled Stallworth all the time. We used two old veteran players and it was a very simple call. The corner covering on the key play of the game, if there is such a thing, when he caught the ball up the middle, was supposed to have Stallworth and we were supposed to have over-the-top help. Well, if you remember the play there was obviously no over-the-top help.

"Now, they had an outstanding team, but once Swann went down I thought, 'We're going to jump all over this.' Unfortunately we blew a call and it cost us a touchdown."

Radakovich, now an assistant coach at Robert Morris University in Pittsburgh, was also asked about his memories of Super Bowl XIV.

"I remember at the end of that third quarter our team ran down to the other side of the field. No one ever mentioned that. Instead of walking, the whole team ran, just like young kids. So they were wired.

"I remember the last interception by Lambert. I remember Billy Waddy being 20 or 30 yards open on the play. It's on the TV. They show it every once in awhile on TV and it shows me yelling in the press box, 'Ray (Malavasi), Waddy was wide open.' There was nobody within 20 or 30 yards of him. He was our best wide receiver. He was our Swann or Stallworth. He threw to the wrong guy, but it was a great play by Lambert. For a middle linebacker, he got deep on that, did a helluva job.

"I remember Cromwell dropping an interception that probably would've iced the game for us.

"The two passes Stallworth caught. I remember that. The inside safety didn't play it right. The corner played it pretty good—Rod Perry—but the safety was a substitute. He wasn't

Did George Perles (left) need to shuttle linebackers in the Super Bowl to call the defensive plays? The Rams coaches say no.

one of our better cover guys. We double-covered Stallworth on both plays because Swann was out of the game. They hit those two hook-and-gos. They were great plays."

Did the Rams steal the Steelers' signals?

"No, no. George Perles put that in the paper. See, I used to steal signals from some teams when I was with the Steelers, so he thought we were stealing his defensive signals and that couldn't have been further from the truth. For one thing, I was up in the box. And the second thing is I had other things to worry about. Normally a line coach is on the sidelines but I was up in the box. No, nobody even looked at what the Steelers were signaling. That was Perles. He was guessing, but he had some logic on that point because he knew I'd done it a few times. Other teams take film of signal-makers and stuff. Schottenheimer was famous for that and then they'd try to steal signals. We never got to that point."

IN THE OWNER'S BOX

With a cast on his foot, Jack Ham moved with his wife, Joanne, into Art Rooney's box for the majority of the game. The Chief had told Ham he was very worried about the outcome, which didn't help Ham's nerves.

"I learned to appreciate the fans a whole lot more because I'm not sure enough Iron Citys would've calmed me down," Ham said. "You have no control over it. That's why I'm sure fans go crazy a lot of times watching us play out there. That was the first time I remember being a spectator at anything other than when you're out of a preseason game. But, especially for a Super Bowl, it was tough on the nerves. Then again, it was the easiest money I ever made."

The Chief didn't relax until Jack Lambert's interception. After the linebacker made the play, the Chief stood up, lit a cigar, and began walking out.

"Where are you going?" asked his son Dan. "The game's not over."

"It is now," said the Chief.

In the Stands

Mike Wagner didn't have a seat in any luxury box. He watched from the stands on a rubber cushion after having the stitches in his hip taken out.

"As the game went on, I realized this was the worst place to be," he said. "I bit off all my nails, which I never do. I was a nervous wreck. It was a great game, but it's no fun sitting up in the stands. The place to be is on the field."

Bob Hice, on the other hand, was thriving. His mom and stepdad had long since moved away, "the second disassociation," Hice said, and the proud member of "Stiller Nation", one of some 40,000 strong at the Rose Bowl, was working on the Rams fans seated in front of him.

"This guy didn't like me waving my Terrible Towel," Hice said. "But after Stallworth scored that touchdown I started swinging it about three inches over his head. I don't know if it was the towel or the wind coming off it but his hair kept blowing up, and so the guy turned around and said, 'Excuse me, sir. Could you quit swinging that thing?'

"I said, 'Thing? This ain't no thing. This is a Terrible Fucking Towel, buddy, and I'm swingin' it.' And then I started swinging it faster and harder. And then Lambert intercepted that pass, and I lit up this big fat joint and the smoke engulfed them. So they got up and left.

"It was time anyway. The game was over."

CHAPTER IX

POSTSCRIPT:
LET'S TALK ABOUT HEROES

"You have to be a little bit bent, when you think about it, to get to the ultimate level of anything."

—Randy Grossman

You're Terry Bradshaw

Art Rooney Jr. thought Terry Bradshaw's turning point came in 1974 when the benched quarterback didn't fall apart as many expected.

"It was his last chance," Rooney said, "and instead of getting bitter or hitting the bottle, he started reading his Bible, grew a great red beard, ran the offense the way it was supposed to be run. I thought it was his finest moment. He was devoted, started throwing the ball like Unitas, really got ahold of himself.

"My dad would have him over for dinner. He'd tell him sincerely, 'You're Terry Bradshaw.' He'd say, 'I've seen Ruth, Man O'War, Dempsey, Ty Cobb. You're right with those guys.'

"Would Bradshaw be as good coming up today? Of course he would. Would Ruth be as good today? Of course he would. You don't have to re-define those kinds of people.

"Chuck Noll was perfect for Bradshaw, just great. Now, I don't know if Terry ever really got into it with Noll, but Noll was just what he needed, the strict professor."

As well as Bradshaw played in Super Bowl XIV, it's difficult to imagine him playing another game that season. He was drained. He needed pills to sleep throughout Super Bowl week, and without pills slept only three hours the night before the game. After the game, he told reporters he might retire.

"I should have," Bradshaw said 25 years later. "Winning Super Bowls is always exhausting, and after that season I was so tired. I can't imagine what it would've felt like with today's media coverage. I do remember thinking, 'OK, four Super Bowls in 10 years. Hmmm. That's pretty good. Move on now? Hmmm. That looks real good.'"

The day after the Super Bowl, Bradshaw met with Jack Lambert and Joe Greene. They talked him out of it.

"I had some options to do some TV and it was the first time I'd ever looked at money over playing," he said. "But that's the fatigue from being under all that pressure of winning Super Bowls because once you set that standard, and you don't make it, you're a failure. And that's hard. That wears a player out."

Bradshaw played three more full seasons with the Steelers before arm trouble forced him to retire after playing one game in 1983. He was inducted into the Hall of Fame in 1989.

INTERESTING CHARACTERS

• Rocky Bleier: "I would say that Lambert was the most interesting teammate. There are really two sides to Jack. As much as he believes in black and white, he's more complex than that. He's a very well-read guy, probably more than anyone else on the team. Very intelligent, very family-oriented, even when he was single. He had great devotion to his father. Yet, Jack was a loner, and sometimes he fueled it. But Jack was never out looking for fights or arguments. He'd find himself in those situations because he was like the gunslinger and would never walk away and would stand up for rights and what was right. He'd call you on it and he would call fans on it, especially when it came to autographs and pushing. "He never turned a kid down. He'd always take care of kids, but it was the adults, especially during that period of time. They wanted to touch him or be a part of him and it just—he didn't want it.

"I wish I had a personality like Jack's because Jack would handle situations the way they should be handled—you know, by what was right. With me, I'm Mr. Nice Guy. You know, 'Oh, whatever you want. Yeah, walk all over me. I don't care. Sorry to offend you.' But not Jack."

• Mike Merriweather (1982-87) on Lambert: "My locker was right next to his and he used to just sit at his locker and smoke and read a book. If you'd say something to him like, 'Hey, what did you think of this play?' He'd walk off and go into the equipment room to be by himself. But on the field he was a great teammate, a great helper and a great person."

• Dwight White: "You had guys with great athletic ability and talent who won over an extended period of time and still have great friendships and camaraderie among themselves. And then many of them went ahead and continued to have successful lives and careers. So the person I think about today is Chuck Beatty (1969-72). He was here the first couple years I was here and then they released him. But Chuck was a very complex person. He had a unique intellect. He's gone on to be a mayor in a small city in Texas, is a top executive in the Boys Scouts of America, which is great stuff, and is just a helluva guy. He's a person to this day I look up to and that I often kick it with, so to speak, in terms of what's going on out here and how we, as middle-age, worldly, African-American men should look at things. Yeah, it would be Chuck Beatty."

• Randy Grossman: "It was such a cast of characters, I don't know how you could pick just one. There were just a lot of strange people. They're all good people but they're all characters. I mean, Noll's a character when you think about it. He's not an ordinary person. Bradshaw's far from the ordinary person. Lambert's far from the ordinary person. I mean you have to be a little bit bent, when you think about it, to get to the ultimate level of anything. You can't be completely balanced. You've got to have some strange quirks and the other thing obviously is the desire to be the best. But a lot of characters, not a whole lot of normal people. Just a great group of guys. It's a shame we didn't win five."

Place in History

The Steelers finished 9-7 in 1980 and didn't make the playoffs for the first time in nine seasons. Their heart and soul—defense and the running game—slipped precipitously. The 1980 Steelers were 12th in the league in overall defense (22nd against the pass) and 15th in rushing.

Joe Greene came up with the slogan "Win one for the thumb in '81," but in Cleveland Stadium, a sign reading, "You'll be sucking your thumb in '81" was hoisted and the Steelers did nothing about it. They lost to the Browns, 27-6. Then the Steelers went 8-8 in '81. They did make the playoffs in 1982, and then again in 1983, but were eliminated in the first game both times. Then Terry Bradshaw retired and the jig was up.

"I don't think as a rookie," Matt Bahr said, "I fully appreciated what we did in 1979 until many years later. I really thought everyone won a Super Bowl at one point, that everyone got a ring at one point. I didn't appreciate what we had until I spent nine years with the Browns and we got so close against the Denver Broncos. It hammered home to me that everything, every bounce, has to go your way just to get to the Super Bowl, let alone win it."

The Steelers entered the 2004 season without having won a title in 24 years. Perhaps there's a price to pay for winning so often in such a short period of time, for having the greatest football dynasty of all time.

Was it the greatest of all time?

"That's for you writing about it or for people talking about it to speculate on," said Jack Ham. "But, yeah, it was team that could win it a number of different ways. There was defense. We could play the physical game or the finesse game. On offense, our passing game with Bradshaw, particularly in those last couple of Super Bowls, was just very, very difficult to stop. Yeah, with what we did there in that period of time, I truly believe we were the best football team of all time."

"Just look at that football team," said John Banaszak. "There were nine Hall of Famers and there very easily could've been nine different egos. We had two wide receivers make the Hall of Fame. Now you hear Terry joke about some of the competition from those guys, but the competition from those guys was to win the football game. There was never any visual or apparent bickering between anybody on that football team. We had a great combination of Hall of Fame superstars to free agents to rookies and second-year men who came in and filled in when they had to."

Because the Steelers didn't win a fifth title in seven years, as the Green Bay Packers had from 1961-67, the comparison will never truly be settled. An unbiased attempt was made by *New York Times* columnist Dave Anderson a few days after Super Bowl XIV.

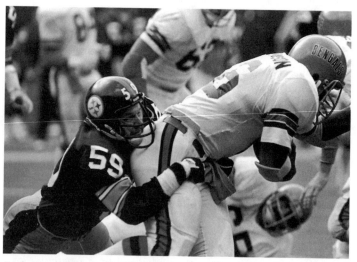

Jack Ham (59) truly believes the Steelers of the 1970s were the greatest football team of all time.

"By their record over the last six seasons and by the evolution of the game and its athletes, these Steelers are the best team in history," Anderson concluded. "They are better than the Green Bay Packers of the 1960s, better than the Cleveland Browns of the '50s, better than the Chicago Bears of the '40s."

Anderson leaned to the Steelers on the strength of their 13-2 won-lost record in postseason play over six years. The Packers were 8-0 in postseason play over seven years, but as Anderson pointed out, the postseason wasn't nearly such a grind in the 1960s.

"But beyond that," he continued, "the Steelers are the best team in NFL history because they are bigger, stronger and faster than those teams were."

A COMPLEX EXPLANATION

Dwight White was once described as complex by Chuck Noll.

"I asked him what he meant by that," White said. "But I didn't stick around for the answer. I didn't really give a shit."

Here's how and why the Steelers dynasty happened, as told by the Mad Dog:

"It was a very unique group of guys coming out of a very unique period. You cannot separate the period and the backgrounds that most of the players came from in coming to Pittsburgh, being the doormat of the NFL. It was a losing scenario and these guys were coming out of this period where the range went from the black movement to the this-is-America-and-you-can-do-anything dream. It was just a different time with Vietnam, civil rights, going to the moon, the war on poverty, fast cars, the sexual revolution. There was a wide range of things going on, and that was part of what was in the heart and soul of each of those guys. They came out of that period and most guys came from a nuclear family. It was a much different environment. We were more traditional in the way we looked at things. Anything was conceivable.

"So that's why when we came to Pittsburgh in 1970 and this whole thing about, 'Well, the Steelers would find a way to lose. They're a terrible team.' These guys refuted that. They'd say, 'You can't be talking about me. You must be talking about those bums from the previous decades.' We were a whole different breed. I think that had so much to do with the mental toughness and the perseverance.

"I'm just emphasizing that I think the time and period that most of us came out of had a lot do with the internal character that it took to win so much. I played 10 years and for nine of those 10 I was in the playoffs and in four Super Bowls. That's more than talent. But there was great, great talent. You could've gotten Elmer Fudd to coach that football team. I'm not suggesting Chuck Noll was Elmer Fudd or something less. He's a very bright man. I've got a lot of respect for Chuck. But I'm telling you, from a talent standpoint, the only thing you had to do, and hear me clearly, was to keep everybody focused, keep everyone from tearing one another apart because you had very high-strung people, very, very strong personalities in there.

"Focus and sense of purpose, as Chuck said, that was the task. Put the muzzles on and take 'em off and say, 'OK guys, go get 'em.'

"Between Monday and Saturday, that was the problem. It was like having 45 rottweilers or pit bulls you had to keep focused and organized and walking the same pace all week long. We did have our characters, the Joe Gilliams and the Ernie Holmes, but still we had enough of the good stuff and focus to stay on top for 10 years."

THE TIGHT MAN

Craig Wolfley is the only member of the Steelers' All-Century Offensive Team who did not play in the 1970s. In a vote by fans in January of 2000, Wolfley was named the Steelers' all-time left guard, and he laughs about it.

"I look at that as the first Y2K glitch," Wolfley said. "There's no doubt in my mind Sam's the all-timer there."

The smile leaves Wolfley's face when the questions continue about Sam Davis.

"It sickens me to think one man would do something like that to another man," Wolfley said.

Sam Davis, the Steelers' offensive captain of the 1970s, was beaten and tortured in his Beaver County home in September of 1991. He was found at the bottom of his stairs and police concluded Davis fell down those stairs. Rumors are rampant that Davis owed the wrong people money, but police said, "The circumstances were not suspicious," according to the *Post-Gazette.*

Davis is still in a personal care home outside of Pittsburgh.

"They used to call him 'Tight Man' because he kept everybody together," Wolfley said. "He was a guy who took me in as a young rookie who was essentially being groomed to take his place, and he shared selflessly with me and would spend a lot of time going over what our job assignments were against particular defenses. He was a terrific player and an excellent leader."

Davis was put on injured reserve in 1980 and replaced at left guard by Ray Pinney. Davis retired after the season and Wolfley played left guard from 1981 through 1989.

"When I was a rookie," Wolfley said, "Sam took me aside one time and said, 'Look, now, you've got to get in your book and you've got to spend a lot of time there. Don't be going out and wasting time on stupid stuff. You've got a job here. And when you run into a brick wall and don't understand something, my room number's such and such. Come on down to my room. We'll sit and go over it.' And we did that probably every other night in my rookie camp.

"I remember when we were going to play against the Dallas Cowboys. He'd always had great battles with Randy White, and he'd tell me, 'Make sure you do this, do that, be strong with the left hand, watch his feet, get a read when he's going inside.' Things of that nature where he went way above and beyond the call of duty as far as sharing with me. So I have the utmost respect for Sam. He's just somebody I love very deeply. He's always been very selfless in what he's shared with all the young guys."

THE LAST HURRAH

The ol' boys came back to close down Three Rivers Stadium on December 16, 2000. The Steelers moved into Heinz Field the following season, but not before Jack Ham, Jack Lambert, Mel Blount and Franco Harris walked to midfield on a rainy Saturday afternoon for the coin toss against the Washington Redskins.

The Steelers won the coin toss and Lambert went off.

"Jack just got fired up," said an emotional Levon Kirkland, the Steelers' captain at the time. "He started yelling, 'All right defense! Let's kill! Let's go!'"

The Steelers won, 24-3.

The four players were joined by several others in a postgame party in the rain, with the fans, that didn't end until Lambert said it did.

Down in the bowels of the stadium, at a small bar this intrepid correspondent for *Steelers Digest* never knew existed, could be found one Jack Lambert. He was holding court with a half-dozen or so former Steelers, telling a story that mocked Terry Hanratty, who was seated nearby with a big smile on his face. Greg Lloyd sat at attention, a rare smile on his face. The bartender, dressed as if he were about to sing in a barbershop quartet, dried the beer mugs with two hands and a big smile on his face. He wasn't watching Lambert, just listening and smiling. All was right once again in his world, in his bar, a bar that probably hadn't been used since the last time Lambert entertained.

Lambert stopped talking to look up at the intruder. I only needed a minute to record his fondest memories for the team paper.

"Sure," he said. "Give me a sec."

So Lambert finished. Hanratty was the butt of the story. They all laughed; Hanratty the loudest. Lambert walked off to the side, down the hall a bit.

"My best memories?" he said. "Well, let's see..."

He wore a beret. The last time I'd looked into the eyes of a man wearing a beret, a man with the same craggy face and piercing look in his eyes was, well, hell, 1979. It was green, too. The beret. He was in Vietnam, I'd supposed. He was a biker now, one of the Pagans. He wanted to know what I was going to do with my life. I was 18 and lived to be 19 because "a writer" must've been the right answer.

"Hey, Jack," a voice interrupted.

It was Lloyd.

"Why are you talking to this asshole? Let's git to that joint you was talkin' about."

Lambert glared at Lloyd the way no one had before, or since, I'd assumed. Told him he had no class and that he'd be there when he was done "talking to this gentleman."

"Where were we?" Lambert asked.

The Chief.

"Right. Probably my fondest memory of being here in Three Rivers Stadium," Lambert continued, "was sitting in Arthur J. Rooney's office the few short times that I did it, and listening to him tell stories about his good friend George Halas and guys like Johnny "Blood" McNally. He knew I loved to hear those stories, and just the thought of sitting in that office alone with him, hearing about the train rides to football games and what it was like in the old days, that's what I take from here."

Would you have liked to have played in this big-buck era?

Jack Lambert (58) was a stand-up guy.

"Well, of course I would," he said. "But when I really would've liked to have played was in the '50s and '60s when men were men. They talk about how rough the game is today, how big and strong they are, but if you watch games from the '50s and '60s, every single time a quarterback goes back to pass, there's roughing the passer. They were clotheslining people and there was no foul. The game now, I see guys getting fined $5,000 for making legitimate tackles on tight ends. My God, if that's a $5,000 fine, I would've donated my salary to the National Football League."

Who was the toughest player you ever faced?

"Probably Mike Webster," Lambert said. "I played against Mike Webster every day in practice, and practice today is not like it was when I played. When Chuck Noll was the coach, we put on our pads Wednesday, Thursday and Friday, and we hit every single day. We did everything but tackle. Did it wear us out? I don't know. But I've got four Super Bowl rings."

Thanks, Jack.

WHERE ARE THEY NOW?

Dirt Winston is in his 13th season of coaching, and for the last three years, as a defensive assistant at the University of Toledo, he's tried to stop Ben Roethlisberger, the current next great thing with the Steelers.

"He *is* the next Bradshaw," Winston said. "Trust me, that young man can play. Put some people around him and he *will* be the next Bradshaw in Pittsburgh."

Is that such a good thing, Terry? After all, Bradshaw avoided Pittsburgh after he retired. He even missed the Chief's funeral in 1988. Bradshaw did come back for the first time in

19 years for a game, and he was so anxious about his reception he brought his daughters onto the field with him.

"For whatever reason, I had this in the back of my mind that people didn't appreciate our efforts, or appreciate me, and I wanted to kind of stick up for myself but I didn't. I just took it in and kind of smothered it," Bradshaw said in a 2004 return. "But after going to all these therapy classes the last few years I found out you best get it out in the open. You'll feel better about yourself."

John Banaszak is selling a digital play analyzer to high school and small college coaches, and in his spare time he's working under Coach Joe Walton and assistant coach Dan Radakovich at Robert Morris University. Banaszak tells the story of his hiring in 2003:

"When I was talking to Joe Walton about the situation, Bad Rad was in California. I asked for the defensive playbook before camp, and Joe said, 'Well, you know, John, Bad Rad doesn't have a playbook.' So I asked for maybe some defensive cut-ups from the previous year to get a feel. Joe said, 'John, you know Bad Rad doesn't have any cut-ups.' OK, maybe I could meet with Bad Rad before training camp to get a feel for the defense and what he wants to get done. 'Well, John, Bad Rad won't be back here until the day before training camp.'

"That's the way they run things, and there is more than one way to run a successful football program. You don't have to put in 20 hours a day. You don't have to sleep in your office. It's basic football. If you can't block, can't tackle, if you can't do the fundamentals, then you can't play. Like Chuck Noll, Bad Rad teaches fundamentals. The scheme is very sound but not excessive. It's very similar to what we did with the Steelers. We're not going to send six people in on third down to run a completely different defense. We didn't shuttle people in and out. We played the same 11 whether it was first down or third down and long. That's the philosophy Joe and Bad Rad have.

You know what we're going to do and if you're better than us, knock us off the ball."

Donnie Shell played 14 years with the Steelers, still holds the unofficial NFL record for interceptions by a strong safety (51) and later obtained a master's degree in guidance and counseling from his beloved South Carolina State. He nearly won another Super Bowl ring in 2003 as the director of player development with the Carolina Panthers.

"I was only with him a couple years," said former Panthers and Steelers safety Brent Alexander. "If you had a rough game, you'd talk to him and everything was right again. He could see every facet of what you were going through."

"The coach's job is to win football games," said Shell, "and to win, football players have to be focused on the field. If their minds are on something else, they're not going to be productive players."

Tom Moore runs perhaps the most explosive offense in the NFL with the Indianapolis Colts. He and Coach Tony Dungy took the Colts to the AFC Championship Game at the end of the 2003 season. The two go back to Dungy's college days at Minnesota. Dungy can't believe Noll's assistants, such as Moore, Dick Hoak, Woody Widenhofer and George Perles, never became pro head coaches.

"I never worried about it," Moore said. "I was always taught to be the best you can be at what you're doing and everything else will take care of itself. I don't feel cheated."

Moore sees plenty of similarities between Noll and Dungy.

"Both of them are great students of the game, very, very smart, intelligent and both of them have a very definite defined way of what it takes to win," he said. "It's coaching, it's teaching, it's fundamentals, it's the basics. That was something Chuck always taught us, you win with fundamentals and techniques. You don't trick people. Those were things Tony believed, and playing for Chuck and coaching for Chuck, I think all those things just reinforced Tony's beliefs. They're very, very similar in their approach to the game, their handling of the team, their handling of game-day operations and total-week preparedness. They're both very, very consistent. There are no highs; there are no lows. It's one steady stream. And they're both tremendous competitors. You don't see it outwardly, but trust me, inwardly it exists and the same with Chuck. Both of them are fierce competitors."

In the 2003 AFC Championship Game, Dungy's receivers were mugged in their pass routes by the Patriots. After the Super Bowl, the NFL warned its coaches the old defensive contact rules would be strictly enforced in 2004. The league called it a "point of emphasis."

"It's kind of like deja vu, only the situation is reversed," said Dungy, who wasn't complaining at the time of the change. He never complained in Tampa where he was on the wrong end of several controversial replay calls. He took that from Noll, too.

"Instead of crying about how those rules changes would hurt Coach Noll's defenses, he looked for ways to exploit it on offense," Dungy said. "Whatever it takes. Remember that? If that's the rule, let's not cry, let's adjust."

John Stallworth is the owner of an aerospace company in Alabama; Larry Brown owns and operates several Applebee franchises in the Pittsburgh area; Jack Lambert has retired as deputy wildlife conservation officer for the Pennsylvania Game Commission in order to raise his four children; Rocky Bleier is in investment banking and motivational speaking; Steve Courson's damaged heart was regenerated through the use of Symbiotropin, an over-the-counter anti-aging supplement that facilitates the body's natural release of human growth hormone; Ted Peterson is the athletic director at Pittsburgh's Upper St. Clair High School; Jack Ham is the president of a drug-testing firm as well as a radio and TV football analyst; Jon Kolb works for Sharon Regional Health

System in its wellness and fitness programs; and Lynn Swann works for ABC Sports.

THE GAME TODAY

The 1979 Steelers were the last team to win an NFL championship with all homegrown talent. Because of free agency, it will probably never happen again. The topic was discussed prior to a fundraiser for Mel Blount's Youth Home.

"We were fortunate to be able to keep these guys together and that makes for success," said Chuck Noll. "You know, you're in there for one or two years, or I guess the maximum is four, then they go someplace else. I don't think it helps the game, personally. I think you need to stay together and work together and get to know one another because it takes time."

"People always equate happiness and everything and the thrill of this game with money," said Terry Bradshaw. "But honestly if I were playing today and I thought my contract was going to disrupt the team, I know that it wouldn't be that big an issue. We didn't have that and I can't imagine going into work this year and knowing that I've got five guys whose contracts were up. There'd be no way Pittsburgh could sign all these players. We'd lose three players for sure, maybe all five. Then you'd start over and rebuild through the draft and then you'd lose them again. I don't see why people even want to coach, knowing you have those kinds of restrictions sitting out there."

"It's real easy to beat up on the players now," said Randy Grossman, "talking about how much money they're making and how much they're looking forward to their next contract, but I think, just as it's always been, the majority of the players are playing because they love playing football. If the salaries were half of what they are, they would still be playing. And if it was a quarter of what they're getting now, they'd still play because the alternatives aren't viable. I mean, teaching is great. Being a police officer is great. Stocking shelves is great, an honorable job. But I mean, this is a gift we've been given for a very short amount of time. It's the exception. It just happens to be the economics of the game that players take advantage of, as we all do in our lines of work. But you've got to love this to get beat up. I mean, money's great but like Chuck said, you pay a significant price. Camp is not fun. Practice is not a whole lot of fun. But you enjoy it and you're young and you're dumb and you do it. I mean, you get to be a kid for a long time."

"People always ask, 'What do you want: the money or the rings?'" said Bradshaw. "Those rings stay with you forever. You'd rather win."

"You know, you want to have fun," said Noll, "and there's no fun losing. Fun comes in winning and you have to have good people who are dedicated and want to pay the price. And then it's fun."

But can't today's free agents simply sign with a winning team? And therefore won't they miss out on the camaraderie these Steelers all enjoyed and are obviously still enjoying?

"You don't know that they'd miss it, though," said John Stallworth. "A lot of these guys have never experienced that. They have played under rules they are playing under now. They've never been with a team on which guys have stayed together for 10, 11 years. They don't know. Their means of comparison is what happened three, four years ago, not 20 years ago. So we can tell them what we had, but they never experienced that."

"Last time they experienced that was in high school," said Grossman. "They didn't even experience it in college because they're coming out early. I mean, the last time they hung out with their buddies, someone they spent a lot of time with, for a long time, was high school. It's different. It's just different."

Dwight White wasn't a part of the roundtable discussion but provided insight into what today's players are missing, because, frankly, they make too much money.

"When I played," White said, "the first year I made $16,000. Football was a stepping stone, an excellent push-off. I worked in the off seasons. You knew you had to work after the game. You knew that. Today, a guy plays six years and he's made $13 million. There's no reason to plan for your life's work, and I think it's foolhardy. It's a big negative today. Football back then gave you a way of meeting people, experiencing a few things, making a few dollars, going a few places. You'd just come off the farm. You ain't been nowhere and football provided all those types of things. Today, football provides a lot more, but the person has no reason to really tap into those things because he stops growing. He's made so much money he really doesn't have to learn how to spell Pennsylvania, because he isn't going to be here anyway.

"That would be a good question in the locker room. Pass a piece of paper around, have them put their number on it and ask them to spell Pittsburgh, Pennsylvania. See how many of them get it right. It's scary to think about the outcome. The human resource department would be asking you what you think you were doing. But seriously, after four games or so, when they're going on about how much they love Pittsburgh and the fans and blah, blah, blah, blah, blah, ask them to put the mayor's name on that piece of paper. If five could do it, I'd be stunned."

THE GREATEST STEELER

In a fan vote at the turn of the century, Joe Greene was named the greatest player in franchise history on 6,920 ballots. Terry

Bradshaw was second (6,681) and Jack Lambert was third (6,542). Greene was uncomfortable with the topic.

"That's debatable," he said. "Everybody on that team needed some help from somebody. You could say it was Terry. Who helped him?"

Franco and the receivers.

"Right, right. Who helped Lambert?"

The guys in front of him, the guys at the side of him, Mel Blount.

"Who helped Mel Blount?"

The safeties, the pass-rushers.

"Who helped me?"

Mel Blount, L.C.

"Right. Ernie. Dwight. Who helped them? See, we were connected. Everybody brought something to the table. That's what it is about a team."

You could say it was the last true team, considering today's rules. Is the lost era lamentable?

"Well, if you're a purist and you're an old-school guy, yeah, probably. But times change and however they're structured you still have to get it done to be a champion. Look at Denver, how they finally got there after a decade of trying to get it done with Elway in the '80s and it didn't happen. But they finally put a group together that understood. New England put together a group that understands what it takes to win. There are no weak sisters on the football team when you win. Everybody makes a contribution. Regardless of what era, it's still team, and I think that's the beauty of this game."

What did you like most about your team?

"The people. The people. The events that occurred while we were together. The challenges that were put in front of us as a group as individuals. The good times that we shared. Growing up together, which was painful at times. All of that. You can look at that in retrospect and say that, yeah, that was good. It didn't feel so good when it was happening, though."

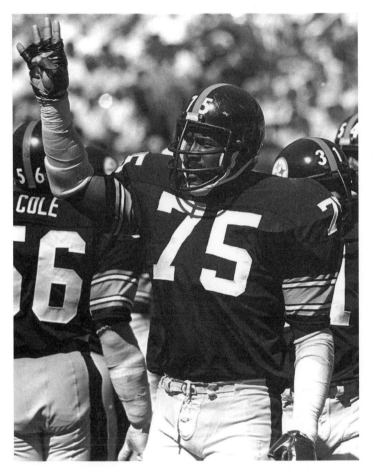

Joe Greene (75) was one of 22 Steelers to earn four Super Bowl rings. According to a vote of fans, he was the greatest of them all.

Was Chuck Noll a taskmaster?

"Not really. Chuck just had an idea of what he thought it would take from the standpoint of commitment, attitude and behavior, what it would take to have success. He never said anything like, 'It's my way or the highway.' He never said anything like that. It was just about having enough guys who believed in him and his methods and tried to emulate him.

"I could assure you that you could get one question, set up a scenario, and you'd ask me how would I respond to it. You could probably ask 12 other guys and they'd probably give you the same answer without it being rehearsed.

"See, if you weren't there, most people attribute it to, well, Noll the taskmaster, the clichés, the bullshit, call it what you want to call it. Fabrications. But the experience of being on the Pittsburgh Steelers for me, from '69 to '81, was a very good experience, and how we went about it with the leadership was how it should be done."

Celebrate the Heroes of Pennsylvania Sports
and Professional Football in These Other 2004 Releases from Sports Publishing!